THE ILLUSTRATED
LONG WALK TO
FREEDOM

THE ILLUSTRATED
LONG WALK TO
FREEDOM

THE AUTOBIOGRAPHY OF NELSON MANDELA

Little, Brown

Dedication

I dedicate this book to my six children, Madiba and Makaziwe (my first daughter), who are now deceased, and to Makgatho, Makaziwe, Zenani and Zindzi, whose support and love I treasure; to my twenty-one grandchildren and three great-grandchildren, who give me great pleasure; and to all my comrades, friends and fellow South Africans whom I serve and whose courage, determination and patriotism remain my source of inspiration.

Acknowledgements

As readers will discover, this book has a long history. I began writing it clandestinely in 1974 during my imprisonment on Robben Island. Without the tireless labour of my old comrades Walter Sisulu and Ahmed Kathrada for reviving my memories, it is doubtful the manuscript would have been completed. The copy of the manuscript which I kept with me was discovered by the authorities and confiscated. However, in addition to their unique calligraphic skills, my co-prisoners Mac Maharaj and Isu Chiba had ensured that the original manuscript safely reached its destination. I resumed work on it after my release from prison in 1990.

Since my release, my schedule has been crowded with numerous duties and responsibilities, which have left me little free time for writing. Fortunately, I have had the assistance of dedicated colleagues, friends and professionals who have helped me complete my work at last, and to whom I would like to express my appreciation. Thanks again to my comrade Ahmed Kathrada for the long hours spent revising, correcting and giving accuracy to the story.

I am deeply grateful to Richard Stengel who collaborated with me in the creation of this book, providing invaluable assistance in editing and revising the first parts and in the writing of the latter parts. I recall with fondness our early morning walks in the Transkei and the many hours of interviews at Shell House in Johannesburg and my home in Houghton. A special tribute is owed to Mary Pfaff who assisted Richard in his work. I have also benefited from the advice and support of Fatima Meer, Peter Magubane, Nadine Gordimer and Ezekiel Mphahlele.

Many thanks to my ANC office staff who patiently dealt with the logistics of the making of this book, but in particular to Barbara Masekela for her efficient co-ordination. Likewise, Iqbal Meer has devoted many hours to watching over the business aspects of the book. I am grateful to my editor, William Phillips of Little, Brown, who has guided this project from early 1990 on, and edited the text. He was ably assisted by Jordan Pavlin and Steve Schneider. I would also like to thank Professor Gail Gerhart for her factual review of the manuscript.

LITTLE, BROWN

This paperback edition first published in 2001
Reprinted 2003, 2004, 2006
This illustrated and abridged edition first published in Great Britain in hardback in 1996 (Original edition published in Great Britain by Little, Brown in hardback in 1994 and in paperback by Abacus in 1995.)

Text copyright © 1994 by Nelson Rolihlahla Mandela
The moral right of the author has been asserted.

For picture acknowledgements see page 208

A CIP catalogue for this book is available form the British Library

ISBN-13:0-316-73312-1
ISBN-10:978-0-316-73312-0

Text abridgement and picture editing by Paul Duncan

Designed by Andrew Barron and Collis Clements Associates

Printed and bound in Italy by Graphicom

Little Brown
An imprint of
Time Warner Book Group UK
Brettenham House
Lancaster Place
London WC2E 7EN
www.twbg.co.uk

Contents

A Country Childhood

The Transkei (opposite) is 800 miles east of Cape Town, 550 miles south of Johannesburg, and lies between the Kei River and the Natal border, between the rugged Drakensberg mountains to the north and the blue waters of the Indian Ocean to the east. It is a beautiful country of rolling hills, fertile valleys, and a thousand rivers and streams which keep the landscape green even in winter. It is home to the Thembu people, who are part of the Xhosa nation, of which I am a member.

We were mostly left to our own devices (below) and played with toys we made ourselves, moulding animals and birds out of clay.

Apart from life, a strong constitution and an abiding connection to the Thembu royal house, the only thing my father bestowed upon me at birth was a name, Rolihlahla. In Xhosa, Rolihlahla literally means 'pulling the branch of a tree', but its colloquial meaning is 'troublemaker'. My more familiar English name was not given to me until my first day of school.

I was born on 18 July 1918 at Mvezo, a tiny village on the banks of the Mbashe River in the district of Umtata, the capital of the Transkei. My father, Gadla Henry Mphakanyiswa, was a chief by both blood and custom. He was confirmed as chief of Mvezo by the king of the Thembu tribe, though under British rule his selection had to be ratified by the government.

According to tradition, the Thembu people migrated from the Drakensberg mountains in the sixteenth century, where they were incorporated into the Xhosa nation. Each Xhosa belongs to a clan that traces its descent back to a specific forefather. I am a member of the Madiba clan, named after a Thembu chief who ruled in the Transkei in the eighteenth century. Stories that I was in the line of succession to the Thembu throne are a myth. Although I was a member of the royal household, I was not among the privileged few who were trained for rule. Instead I was groomed, like my father before me, to counsel the rulers of the tribe.

In later years, I discovered that my father was not only an adviser to kings but a kingmaker. After the untimely death of Jongilizwe in the 1920s, a dispute arose as to who should be selected to succeed him. My father was consulted and recommended Jongintaba on the grounds that he was the best educated. In time, Jongintaba would return the favour.

My father had four wives, the third of whom was my mother, Nosekeni Fanny, the daughter of Nkedama from the amaMpemvu clan of the Xhosa. My father sired thirteen children in all, four boys and nine girls, and I am the youngest son. My father's heir as chief was Daligqili, the son of the Great House, who died in the early 1930s.

When I was an infant, my father was involved in a dispute that deprived him of his chieftainship. My father possessed a proud rebelliousness, a stubborn sense of fairness, that I recognize in myself. As a chief he was compelled to account not only to the Thembu king but to the local magistrate. One day, he asserted his traditional prerogative as a chief and challenged the authority of the magistrate over some tribal matter. Such behaviour was regarded as the height of insolence. The magistrate simply deposed my father, thus ending the Mandela family chieftainship. As a result, my father, who was a wealthy nobleman by the standards of his time, lost both his fortune and his title. My mother then moved to Qunu, north of Mvezo, where she would have the support of friends and relations.

The village of Qunu was situated in a narrow, grassy valley. It consisted of a few hundred people who lived in huts, grouped some distance away from the fields. There were no roads, only paths through the grass. Cattle, sheep, goats and horses grazed together in common pastures.

Our diet mostly consisted of maize (mealies), sorghum, beans and pumpkins, largely because people could not afford anything else. The water used for farming, cooking and washing had to be fetched in buckets from streams and springs. This was women's work and, indeed, Qunu was a village of women and children: most of the men spent the greater part of the year working on farms or in the mines along the Reef. They returned perhaps twice a year, mainly to plough their fields. The hoeing, weeding and harvesting were left to the women and children.

My mother presided over three huts at Qunu: one was used for cooking, one for sleeping and one for storage. There was no furniture in the Western sense. We slept on mats and sat on the ground. My mother cooked food in a three-legged iron pot over an open fire in the centre of the hut or outside. Everything we ate we grew and made ourselves.

From an early age, I spent most of my free time in the veld playing and fighting with the other boys of the village. We were mostly left to our own devices. We played with toys we made ourselves, moulding animals and birds out of clay and building ox-drawn sledges out of tree branches. At the end of the day, I would return to my mother's kraal where she was preparing supper. Whereas my father told stories of historic battles and heroic warriors, my mother would enchant us with Xhosa legends and fables that had come down from numberless generations. These tales stimulated my childish imagination, and usually contained some moral lesson.

The only rivalry between different clans or tribes at Qunu was that between the Xhosas and the amaMfengu. The amaMfengu were the most advanced section of the community, among the first to become Christians, to build better houses and to use scientific methods of agriculture, and they were wealthier than the Xhosa.

An elaborate demonstration
of stick-fighting – essential
knowledge to any rural
African boy. I became
adept at its various
techniques, parrying blows,
feinting in one direction
and striking in another,
breaking away from an
opponent with quick
footwork. From these days I
date my love of the veld, of
open spaces, the simple
beauties of nature, the
clean line of the horizon.

In Qunu the women and children of the village wore blankets dyed with ochre; only the few Christians in the village wore Western-style clothing.

My father befriended two amaMfengu brothers, George and Ben Mbekela, who were educated and Christian. While the faith of the Mbekela brothers did not rub off on my father, it did inspire my mother, who became a Christian. It was due to their influence that I was baptized into the Methodist Church and sent to school. One day, George Mbekela paid a visit to my mother. 'Your son is a clever young fellow,' he said. 'He should go to school.' No one in my family had ever attended school, but my father, despite his own lack of education, immediately decided that his youngest son should go to school.

On the first day of school my teacher, Miss Mdingane, gave each of us an English name. This was the custom among Africans in those days and was undoubtedly due to the British bias of our education. That day, Miss Mdingane told me that my new name was Nelson. Why this particular name I have no idea.

When I was nine years old, my father died. I do not remember experiencing great grief so much as feeling cut adrift. After a brief period of mourning, my mother informed me that I would be leaving Qunu. I did not ask her why, or where I was going.

I packed the few things that I possessed and early one morning we set out westward. I mourned less for my father than for the world I was leaving behind. Qunu was all that I knew, and I loved it in the unconditional way that a child loves his first home. Before we disappeared behind the hills, I turned and looked for what I imagined was the last time at my village.

We travelled in silence until the sun was sinking slowly towards the horizon. It was an exhausting journey, along rocky dirt roads, up and down hills, past numerous villages, but we did not pause. Late in the afternoon, at the bottom of a shallow valley surrounded by trees, we came upon a village at the centre of which was a large and gracious home. It so far exceeded anything I had ever seen that all I could do was marvel at it. It consisted of two houses and seven stately rondavels (huts), surrounded by spacious gardens. Encircling the property was a

At tribal meetings (right) a group of councillors of high rank functioned as parliament and judiciary. They were wise men who retained the knowledge of history and custom in their heads and whose opinions carried great weight.

Chief Jongintaba (below) acting regent of the Thembu people. His name suited him, for Jongintaba literally means 'One who looks at the mountains', and he was a man with a sturdy presence upon whom all eyes gazed. He had a dark complexion and an intelligent face.

herd of at least fifty cattle and perhaps five hundred sheep. It was a vision of wealth and order beyond my imagination.

This was the Great Place, Mqhekezweni, the provisional capital of Thembuland, the royal residence of Chief Jongintaba Dalindyebo, acting regent of the Thembu people. As I contemplated all this grandeur an enormous motor car rumbled through the gate. Out of the car stepped a short, thickset man wearing a smart suit. He had the confidence and bearing of a man who was used to the exercise of authority. This was the regent, who was to become my guardian and benefactor for the next decade.

I learned later that, after my father's death, Jongintaba had offered to become my guardian. He would treat me as he treated his other children, and I would have the same advantages as they. My mother had no choice; one did not turn down such an offer. The regent had not forgotten that it was due to my father that he had become acting paramount chief.

My mother remained in Mqhekezweni for a day or two before returning to Qunu. Children are often the least sentimental of creatures, especially if they are absorbed in some new pleasure. Even as my mother was leaving, my head was swimming with the delights of my new home.

I was quickly caught up in the daily life of Mqhekezweni. When I was not in school, I was a ploughboy, a waggon guide, a shepherd. I rode horses and shot birds with slingshots and found boys to joust with, and some nights I danced the evening away to the beautiful singing and clapping of Thembu maidens. Although I missed Qunu and my mother, I was completely absorbed in my new world.

I was no more than five when I became a herd-boy looking after sheep and calves in the fields. It was there that I learned how to knock birds out of the sky with a slingshot, to gather wild honey and fruits and edible roots, to drink warm, sweet milk straight from the udder of a cow, to swim in the clear, cold streams, and to catch fish with twine and sharpened bits of wire.

I attended a one-room school next door to the palace and studied English, Xhosa, history and geography. We read *Chambers English Reader* and did our lessons on black slates. Our teachers took a special interest in me. I did well in school not so much through cleverness as through doggedness. My own self-discipline was reinforced by my aunt Phathiwe, who lived in the Great Place and scrutinized my homework every night.

If the world of Mqhekezweni revolved around the regent, my smaller world revolved around his two children. Justice, the elder, was his only son and heir to the Great Place, and Nomafu was the regent's daughter. I lived with them and was treated exactly as they were. We ate the same food, wore the same clothes, performed the same chores. We were later joined by Nxeko, the older brother to Sabata, the heir to the throne. The four of us formed a royal quartet.

Justice was four years older than me and became my first hero after my father. I looked up to him in every way. He was already at Clarkebury, a boarding school about sixty miles away. Justice and I became the best of friends, though we were opposites in many ways: he was extroverted, I was introverted; he was lighthearted, I was serious. Things came easily to him; I had to drill myself.

At Qunu, the only time I had ever attended church was on the day that I was baptized. Religion was a ritual that I indulged in for my mother's sake and to which I attached no meaning. But at Mqhekezweni, religion was a part of the fabric of life and I attended church each Sunday along with the regent and his wife.

Because of the universal respect the regent enjoyed – from both black and white – and the seemingly untempered power that he wielded, I saw chieftaincy as being the very centre around which life revolved. My later notions of leadership were profoundly influenced by observing the regent and his court. I watched and learned from the tribal meetings that were regularly held at the Great Place. These were called to discuss national matters such as a drought, the culling of cattle, policies ordered by the magistrate, or new laws decreed by the government. All Thembus were free to come – and a great many did, on horseback or by foot.

The Drakensberg mountains. According to tradition, the Thembu people lived in the foothills of the Drakensberg mountains and migrated towards the coast in the sixteenth century, when they were incorporated into the Xhosa nation.

The night before the circumcision, there was a ceremony with singing and dancing, and we forgot for the moment what lay ahead. At dawn, we were escorted to the river to bathe. Circumcision is a trial of bravery and stoicism; a man must suffer in silence. I felt as if fire was shooting through my veins; the pain was so intense that I buried my chin in my chest. We were looked after by a guardian, who explained the rules we had to follow if we were to enter manhood properly. He painted our naked and shaved bodies from head to foot in white ochre, symbolizing our purity. We were then instructed to bury our foreskins. The traditional reason for this practice was so that they would be hidden before wizards could use them for evil purposes, but, symbolically, we were also burying our youth. We lived in our two huts while our wounds healed. Outside, we were covered in blankets, for we were not allowed to be seen by women. It was a period of quietude, a kind of spiritual preparation for the trials of manhood that lay ahead.

On these occasions, the regent was surrounded by a group of councillors of high rank who functioned as parliament and judiciary. They were wise men who retained the knowledge of tribal history and custom in their heads and whose opinions carried great weight.

Everyone who wanted to speak did so. It was democracy in its purest form. There may have been a hierarchy of importance among the speakers, but everyone was heard: chief and subject, warrior and medicine man, shopkeeper and farmer, landowner and labourer. The foundation of self-government was that all men were free to voice their opinions and were equal as citizens. (Women, I am afraid, were deemed second-class citizens.)

Only at the end of the meeting, as the sun was setting, would the regent speak. His purpose was to sum up what had been said and form some consensus among the diverse opinions. But no conclusion was forced on people who disagreed. If no agreement could be reached, another meeting would be held. At the very end of the council, a praise-singer or poet would deliver a panegyric to the ancient kings.

It was at Mqhekezweni that I developed my interest in African history. Until then I had

heard only of Xhosa heroes, but at the Great Place I learned of other African heroes like Sekhukhune, king of the Bapedi, the Basotho king, Moshoeshoe, and Dingane, king of the Zulus, and others such as Bambatha, Hintsa and Makana, Montshiwa and Kgama. I learned of these men from the chiefs and headmen who came to the Great Place to settle disputes and try cases.

The most ancient of the chiefs who regaled the gathered elders with ancient tales was Zwelibhangile Joyi, a son from the Great House of King Ngubengcuka. Chief Joyi was the great authority on the history of the Thembus, in large part because he had lived through so much of it.

Chief Joyi railed against the white man, whom he believed had deliberately sundered the Xhosa tribe, dividing brother from brother. Chief Joyi said that the African people lived in relative peace until the coming of the *abelungu*, the white people, who arrived from across the sea with fire-breathing weapons. Once, he said, the Thembu, the Pondo, the Xhosa, and the Zulu were all children of one father, and lived as brothers. The white man shattered the *abantu*, the fellowship, of the various tribes. The white man was hungry and greedy for land, and the black man shared the land with him as they shared the air and water; land was not for man to possess. But the white man took the land as you might seize another man's horse.

When I was sixteen, the regent decided that it was time that I became a man. In Xhosa tradition, this is achieved through one means only: circumcision. An uncircumcised male cannot be heir to his father's wealth, cannot marry or officiate in tribal rituals. It is not just a surgical procedure, but a lengthy and elaborate ritual in preparation for manhood.

The traditional ceremony of the circumcision school was arranged principally for Justice. The rest of us, twenty-six in all, were there mainly to keep him company. Early in the new year, we journeyed to two grass huts in a secluded valley on the banks of the Mbashe River, known as Tyhalarha, the traditional place of circumcision for Thembu kings. The huts were seclusion lodges, where we were to live isolated from society. It was a sacred time; I felt happy and fulfilled taking part in my people's customs and ready to make the transition from boyhood to manhood.

At the end of our seclusion, a great ceremony was held to welcome us as men to society. Our families, friends and local chiefs gathered for speeches, songs and gift-giving.

The main speaker was Chief Meligqili, the son of Dalindyebo. He began by remarking how fine it was that we were continuing a long tradition. Then his tone suddenly changed. 'There sit our sons,' he said, 'the flower of the Xhosa tribe, the pride of our nation. We have just circumcised them in a ritual that promises them manhood, but it is a promise that can never be fulfilled. For we Xhosas, and all black South Africans, are a conquered people. We are slaves in our own country. We are tenants on our own soil. We have no strength, no power, no control over our own destiny in the land of our birth. Among these young men are chiefs who will never rule because we have no power to govern ourselves; soldiers who will never fight for we have no weapons to fight with; scholars who will never teach because we have no place for them to study. The abilities, the intelligence, the promise of these young men will be squandered in their attempt to eke out a living doing the simplest, most mindless chores for the white man. These gifts today are naught, for we cannot give them the greatest gift of all, which is freedom and independence.'

Without exactly understanding why, his words began to work on me. He had sown a seed, and though I let that seed lie dormant for a long season, it eventually began to grow.

Unlike most of the others with whom I had been at circumcision school, I was not destined to work in the gold mines on the Reef. My destiny was to become a counsellor to Sabata, and for that I had to be educated. I returned to Mqhekezweni after the ceremony, but not for long, for I was about to cross the Mbashe River.

Founded in 1825, the Clarkebury Institute was both a secondary school and a teacher-training college, and was the highest institution of learning for Africans in Thembuland. The regent himself had attended Clarkebury, and Justice had followed him there. It was a Thembu college, founded on land given by the great Thembu king Ngubengcuka; as a descendant of Ngubengcuka I presumed that I would be accorded the same deference at Clarkebury that I had come to expect in Mqhekezweni. But I was painfully mistaken, for I was treated no differently from everyone else. Plenty of the boys had distinguished lineages, and I was no longer unique. I quickly realized that I had to make my way on the basis of my ability, not my heritage.

My time at Clarkebury broadened my horizons, yet I would not say that I was an entirely unprejudiced young man when I left. I had met students from all over the Transkei, as well as a few from Johannesburg and Basutoland, as Lesotho was then known, some of whom were sophisticated and cosmopolitan. Yet I did not envy them. Even as I left Clarkebury, I was still, at heart, a Thembu, and I was proud to think and act like one. My roots were my destiny, and I believed that I would become a counsellor to the Thembu king, as my guardian wanted.

In 1937, when I was nineteen, I joined Justice at Healdtown, the Wesleyan College in Fort Beaufort, about 175 miles southwest of Umtata. Healdtown attracted students from all over the country, as well as from the protectorates of Basutoland, Swaziland and Bechuanaland. Though it was a mostly Xhosa institution, there were also students from different tribes. After school and at weekends, students from the same tribe kept together. I adhered to this same pattern, but it was at Healdtown that I made my first Sotho-speaking friend, Zachariah Molete. I remember feeling quite bold at having a friend who was not a Xhosa, though our biology teacher was also Sotho-speaking.

I enjoyed myself on the playing fields. The quality of sports at Healdtown was far

Before I went up to university, the regent bought me my first suit. Double-breasted and grey, the suit made me feel grown-up and sophisticated.

superior to that of Clarkebury. During my second year my friend Locke Ndzamela, Healdtown's champion hurdler, encouraged me to take up a new sport: long-distance running. I enjoyed the discipline and solitariness of long-distance running, which allowed me to escape from the hurly-burly of school life. At the same time, I also took up a sport that I seemed less suited for, and that was boxing. Only years later, when I had put on a few more pounds, did I begin to box in earnest.

Until 1960, the University College of Fort Hare in the municipality of Alice, about twenty miles due east from Healdtown, was the only residential centre of higher education for blacks in South Africa. Fort Hare was more than that: it was a beacon for African scholars from all over Southern, Central and Eastern Africa. For young black South Africans like myself, it was Oxford and Cambridge, Harvard and Yale, all rolled into one. The regent was anxious for me to attend Fort Hare and I was pleased to be accepted there. Before I went up to the university, the regent bought me my first suit. Double-breasted and grey, the suit made me feel grown-up and sophisticated.

Fort Hare had only 150 students, and I already knew a dozen or so of them from Clarkebury and Healdtown. One of them was my nephew K.D. Matanzima, a third-year student who took me under his wing. We were both Methodists, and I was assigned to his hostel, known as Wesley House, a pleasant two-storey building on the edge of the campus. Under his tutelage, I attended church services at nearby Loveday, took up soccer (at which he excelled), and generally followed his advice. The regent did not believe in sending money to his children at school, and I would have had empty pockets had not K.D. shared his allowance with me. Like the regent, he saw my future role as counsellor to Sabata, and he encouraged me to study law.

Fort Hare had been founded in 1916 by Scottish missionaries on the site of what was the largest nineteenth-century frontier fort in the eastern Cape. Built on a rocky platform and moated by the winding arc of the Tyume River, Fort Hare was perfectly situated to enable the British to fight the gallant Xhosa warrior Sandile, the last Rharhabe king, who was defeated by the British in one of the final frontier battles in the 1800s.

In my first year, I studied English, anthropology, politics, native administration and Roman Dutch law. Although K.D. was counselling me to study law, I had my heart set on being an interpreter or a clerk in the Native Affairs Department. At that time, a career as a civil servant was a glittering prize for an African, the highest that a black man could aspire to.

My education at Fort Hare was as much outside as inside the classroom. I was a more active sportsman than I had been at Healdtown and was able to compete in both soccer and cross-country running. Running taught me valuable lessons. In cross-country competition, training counted more than intrinsic ability, and I could compensate for a lack of natural aptitude with diligence and discipline.

I became a member of the Students Christian Association and taught Bible classes on Sundays in neighbouring villages. One of my comrades on these expeditions was a serious young science scholar. He came from Pondoland, in the Transkei, and his name was Oliver Tambo. From the start, I saw that Oliver's intelligence was diamond-edged; he was a keen debater and did not accept the platitudes that so many of us automatically subscribed to. Though I did not have much contact with him at Fort Hare, it was easy to see that he was destined for great things.

As a BA, I would finally be able to restore to my mother the wealth and prestige that she had lost after my father's death. I would build her a proper home in Qunu, with a garden and modern furniture and fittings. I would support her and my sisters so that they could afford the things that they had so long been denied. This was my dream and it seemed within reach.

During the second year, I was nominated to stand for the Student Representative Council. Before the election, a meeting of all students was held to discuss problems and voice grievances. The students felt that the diet at Fort Hare was unsatisfactory and that the powers of the SRC needed to be increased. I agreed with both motions, and when a majority of students voted to boycott the elections unless the authorities accepted our demands, I voted with them.

The majority of the students boycotted the election, but twenty-five, about one-sixth of the student body, showed up and elected six representatives, one of whom was myself. We unanimously decided to tender our resignations on the ground that we supported the boycott and did not enjoy the support of the majority of the students. We then drafted a letter, which we handed to Dr Kerr.

But Dr Kerr was clever. He accepted our resignations and then announced that new elections were to be held the next day at suppertime. This would ensure that all the students would be present and that there would be no excuse that the SRC did not have the support of the entire student body. The election was held, as the principal ordered, but only the same twenty-five voted, returning the same six SRC members. It would seem that we were back where we started.

But this time, my five colleagues believed we should now accept office. I countered that nothing had changed; while all the students had been there, a majority of them had not

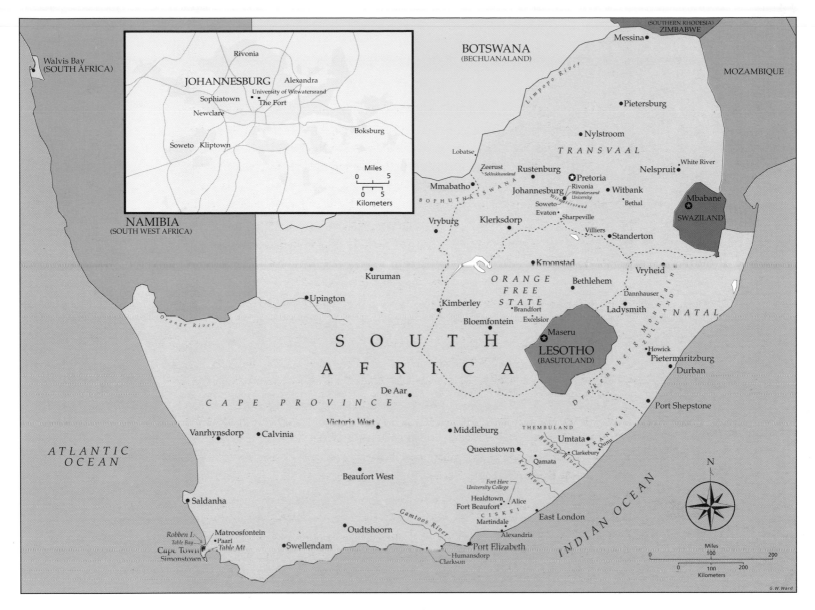

voted, and it would be morally incorrect to say that we enjoyed their confidence. Since our initial goal was to boycott the election, our duty was still to abide by that resolution, and not be deterred by some trickery on the part of the principal. I again resigned.

The following day I was called in to see the principal who asked me to reconsider my decision. He told me to sleep on it, but warned me that if I insisted on resigning, he would have to expel me.

I was shaken by what he had said and spent a restless night. Was I sabotaging my academic career over an abstract moral principle that mattered very little? I had taken a stand, and I did not want to appear to be a fraud in the eyes of my fellow students. At the same time, I did not want to throw away my career at Fort Hare.

The next morning I told Dr Kerr that I could not in good conscience serve on the SRC. He seemed a bit taken aback. 'Very well,' he said. 'It is your decision, of course. You may return to Fort Hare next year provided you join the SRC. You have all summer to consider it, Mr Mandela.'

I was, in a way, as surprised as Dr Kerr. I knew it was foolhardy to leave Fort Hare, but when I needed to compromise, something inside would not let me. While I appreciated Dr Kerr's willingness to give me another chance, I resented his absolute power over my fate. I should have had every right to resign from the SRC if I wished. When I left Fort Hare at the end of the year, I was in an unpleasant state of limbo.

When I told the regent what had transpired he was furious, and could not comprehend the reasons for my actions. He bluntly informed me that I would obey the principal's instructions and return to Fort Hare in the autumn. It would have been pointless as well as disrespectful for me to argue with my benefactor.

Justice had also returned to Mqhekezweni. No matter how long Justice and I were apart, the brotherly bonds that united us were instantly renewed. He had left school the year before and was living in Cape Town.

Within a few days, I resumed my old life at home. I did not dwell on the situation at Fort Hare, but life has a way of forcing decisions on those who vacillate. It was an entirely different matter that forced my hand.

A few weeks after my homecoming, the regent summoned Justice and me to a meeting. 'My children,' he said in a very sombre tone, 'I fear that I am not much longer for this world, and before I journey to the land of the ancestors, it is my duty to see my two sons properly married. I have, accordingly, arranged unions for both of you.'

This announcement took us both by surprise, and Justice and I looked at each other with a mixture of shock and helplessness. The two girls came from very good families, the regent said. Justice was to marry the daughter of Khalipa, a prominent Thembu nobleman, and I was to marry the daughter of the local Thembu priest. The marriages were to take place immediately. Justice and I walked out of our interview with our heads down, dazed and dejected. The regent was acting in accordance with Thembu law and custom, and his own motives could not be impugned: he wanted us to be settled during his lifetime. We had always known that he had the right to arrange marriages for us, but now it was no longer an abstract possibility.

I could not go through with this marriage, which I considered unfair and ill-advised. At the same time, I could no longer remain under the regent's guidance if I rejected his plan for me. Justice agreed, and the two of us decided that the only choice remaining was to run away to Johannesburg.

The regent was preparing to leave to attend a session of the Bungha, the Transkeian legislative assembly, and we decided this was the ideal time to steal away. I had few clothes, and we managed to fit whatever we had into a single suitcase.

We had almost no money between us, but we went to see a local trader and sold him two of the regent's prize oxen. He paid us a very good price, and with the money we hired a car to take us to the local station where we would catch a train.

We managed to get a train to Queenstown. In the 1940s, travelling for an African was a complicated process. All Africans over the age of sixteen were compelled to carry 'Native passes'. Justice and I had our passes in order, but for an African to leave his magisterial district and enter another he also needed travel documents, a permit and a letter from his employer or, in our case, guardian – none of which we had. Our plan was to go to the house of a relative in Queenstown and arrange the necessary documents.

At the house we met Chief Mpondombini, a brother of the regent, who was fond of Justice and myself. Chief Mpondombini greeted us warmly, and we explained that we needed travel documents from the local magistrate, claiming that we were on an errand for the regent. The Chief not only escorted us to the magistrate, but vouched for us and explained our predicament. But the magistrate said that, as a matter of courtesy, he ought to inform the chief magistrate of Umtata, in whose jurisdiction we fell. As luck would have it, the regent was just then paying a call on the chief magistrate of Umtata and was in his very office.

When the regent heard what we were requesting, he exploded, and ordered the magistrate to arrest us. The magistrate regarded us angrily. 'You boys are thieves and liars,' he told us. 'You have presumed upon my good offices and then deceived me. Now I am going to have you arrested.'

I immediately rose to our defence. We had told him lies, that was true. But we had committed no offence and violated no laws, and we could not be arrested simply on the recommendation of a chief, even if he happened to be our father. The magistrate backed down, but told us to leave his office and never to darken his door again.

Justice remembered that he had a friend in Queenstown named Sidney Nxu who was working in the office of a white attorney. We went to see him and explained our situation; he told us that the mother of the attorney was driving into Johannesburg and would give us a ride if we paid a fee of £15 sterling. This was a vast sum, which virtually depleted our savings, but we had no choice. We decided to risk getting the correct travel documents once we were in Johannesburg.

Arriving at about ten o'clock that evening, we saw before us, glinting in the distance, a maze of lights that seemed to stretch in all directions. I was terribly excited to see the city I had heard about since I was a child. Johannesburg had always been depicted as a city of dreams, a city of danger and of opportunity. I remembered the stories we had heard at school, of sleek motor cars, beautiful women and dashing gangsters. It was the city of gold, where I would soon be making my home. I had reached the end of what seemed like a long journey, but it was actually the very beginning of a much longer and more trying journey that would test me in ways that I could not then have imagined.

Johannesburg

It was dawn when we reached the offices of Crown Mines, on a great hill overlooking the still, dark metropolis. Johannesburg had been built up around the discovery of gold on the Witwatersrand in 1886, and Crown Mines was the largest gold mine in the city of gold. I expected to see a grand building like the government offices in Umtata, but the Crown Mine offices were rusted tin shanties.

Gold-mining on the Witwatersrand was costly because the ore was low grade and deep under the earth. Only cheap labour in the form of thousands of Africans working long hours for little pay made gold-mining profitable for the mining houses. It was my first sight of South African capitalism at work, and I knew I was in for a new kind of education.

We went straight to the headman, Piliso, who knew about Justice, as the regent had sent a letter months before making arrangements for him to get a clerical job, the most coveted and respected job in the mine compound. Justice explained that I was his brother. Piliso took me on as a mine policeman, saying that if I worked well, he would give me a clerical post in three months' time.

Many of the miners, especially those from Thembuland, treated Justice as a chief and greeted him with gifts of cash, the custom when a chief visited a mine. Most of these men were in the same hostel; miners were normally housed according to tribe. The mining companies preferred such segregation because it prevented different ethnic groups from uniting around a common grievance.

I started work immediately as a night watchman. The job was a simple one: I waited at the compound entrance next to the sign that read, 'BEWARE: NATIVES CROSSING HERE', and checked the credentials of all those entering and leaving.

Our spell at the mines did not last long. Once our secret had been discovered (we could not resist boasting about our cleverness) we were soon thrown out, and found ourselves without jobs, prospects or somewhere to stay.

I arranged to stay with one of my cousins, Garlick Mbekeni, in George Goch, a small township in southern Johannesburg. Garlick was a friendly, solicitous man, and after I had been there a short while, I told him that my real aspiration was to be a lawyer. He commended me for my ambition and said he would think about what I had said.

A few days later, Garlick told me that he was taking me to see 'one of our best people in Johannesburg'. We took the train to the office of an estate agent in Market Street, a dense and rollicking thoroughfare.

Garlick and I sat in the estate agent's waiting room while a pretty African receptionist announced our presence to her boss in the inner office. She soon ushered us into the inner office, where I was introduced to a man who looked to be in his late twenties, with an intelligent and kindly face, light in complexion, and dressed in a double-breasted suit. To judge from his well-populated waiting room and his desk piled high with papers, he was a busy and successful man. But he did not rush us and seemed genuinely interested in our errand.

Walter Sisulu's name was becoming prominent as both a businessman and a local leader. He paid close attention as I explained my difficulties and my ambition to be a lawyer. When I had finished, he mentioned that there was a white lawyer named Lazar Sidelsky, whom he believed to be a decent and progressive fellow. He would talk to him about taking me on as an articled clerk.

After a brief time with my cousin, I arranged to move in with the Reverend J. Mabutho of the Anglican Church at his home in Eighth Avenue in Alexandra township. Reverend Mabutho was a fellow Thembu, a friend of my family, and a generous, God-fearing man. As a Thembu who knew my family, Reverend Mabutho felt responsible for me. 'Our ancestors have taught us to share,' he once told me.

I then found accommodation with his next-door neighbours, the Xhoma family. Mr Xhoma was one of an elite handful of African landowners in Alexandra. His house was small, particularly as he had six children, but it was pleasant, with a veranda and a tiny garden. In order to make ends meet, Mr Xhoma, like so many other residents of Alexandra, rented rooms to boarders. He had built a tin-roofed room at the back of his property, no more than a shack, with a dirt floor, no heat, no electricity, no running water. But it was a place of my own and I was happy to have it.

In the meantime, on Walter's recommendation, Lazar Sidelsky had agreed to take me on as a clerk while I completed my BA degree. The firm of Witkin, Sidelsky and Eidelman, one of the largest law firms in the city, handled business from blacks as well as whites. In

Despite his youth, he seemed to me an experienced man of the world. He was from the Transkei, but spoke English with a rapid urban fluency. His name was Walter Sisulu.

Sisulu's office specialized in properties for Africans. In the 1940s, there were still quite a few areas where freehold properties could be purchased by Africans, smallholdings located in such places as Alexandra and Sophiatown. In some of these areas, Africans had owned their own homes for several generations.

addition to studying law and passing certain exams, in order to qualify as an attorney in South Africa I would have to serve several years of apprenticeship to a practising lawyer, which is known as serving articles. But I first had to complete my BA degree. To that end, I was studying at night with UNISA, short for the University of South Africa, a respected educational institution that offered degrees by correspondence.

In addition to trying conventional law cases, Witkin, Sidelsky and Eidelman oversaw property transactions for African customers. Walter brought the firm clients who needed a mortgage. The firm would handle their loan applications, and then take a commission, which it would split with the estate agent. In fact, the law firm would take the lion's share of the money, leaving only a pittance for the African estate agent. Even so, the law firm was far more liberal than most. The fact that Lazar Sidelsky, one of the firm's partners, would take on a young African as an articled clerk — something almost unheard-of in those days — was evidence of that liberalism.

I met most of the firm's staff on my first day in the office, including the one other African employee, Gaur Radebe, with whom I shared an office. Ten years my senior, Gaur was a clerk, interpreter and messenger. He was a short, stocky, muscular man, fluent in English, Sotho and Zulu, and expressing himself in all of them with precision, humour and confidence. He had strong opinions and even stronger arguments to back them up and was a well-known figure in black Johannesburg.

As a combination of a clerk and a messenger, I would find, arrange and file documents and serve or deliver papers around Johannesburg. Later, I would draw up contracts for some of the firm's African clients. Yet, no matter how small the job, Mr Sidelsky would explain to me what it was for and why I was doing it. He was a patient and generous teacher, and sought to impart not only the details of the law but the philosophy behind it.

While Mr Sidelsky imparted his views of the law, he warned me against politics. It was

From 1939 South Africa was supplying men and goods to the war effort. Demand for labour was high, and Johannesburg became a magnet for Africans from the countryside seeking work. Between 1941, when I arrived, and 1946, the number of Africans in the city would double. Every morning, the township felt larger than it had the day before. Men found jobs in factories and housing in the 'non-European townships' of Newclare, Martindale, George Goch, Alexandra, Sophiatown and the Western Native Township (below).

the source of trouble and corruption, and should be avoided at all costs. He painted a frightening picture of what would happen to me if I drifted into politics, and counselled me to avoid the company of men he regarded as troublemakers and rabble-rousers, specifically Gaur Radebe and Walter Sisulu.

Gaur was indeed a 'troublemaker', in the best sense of that term, and was an influential man in the African community in ways that Mr Sidelsky did not know or suspect. He was a member of the Advisory Board in the Western Native Township, an elected body of four local people who dealt with the authorities on matters relating to the townships. While it had little power, the board had great prestige among the people. Gaur was also, as I soon discovered, a prominent member of both the ANC and the Communist Party.

Life in Alexandra was exhilarating and precarious. It was desperately overcrowded; every square foot was occupied by either a ramshackle house or a tin-roofed shack. As so often happens in desperately poor places, the worst elements came to the fore. Life was cheap; the gun and the knife ruled at night. Police raids were a regular feature of life in Alexandra. People were routinely arrested for pass violations, possession of liquor and failure to pay the poll tax. On almost every corner there were shebeens, illegal saloons where home-brewed beer was served.

It was also a kind of heaven. As one of the few areas of the country where Africans could acquire

Alexandra occupies a treasured place in my heart. It was the first place I ever lived away from home. Even though I was later to live in Orlando, a small section of Soweto, for a far longer period, I always regarded Alexandra Township as a home where I had no specific house, and Orlando as a place where I had a house but no home.

freehold property and run their own affairs, where people did not have to kowtow to the tyranny of white municipal authorities, Alexandra was an urban Promised Land, evidence that a section of our people had broken their ties with the rural areas and become permanent city-dwellers. The government, in order to keep Africans in the countryside or working in the mines, maintained that Africans were by nature a rural people, ill suited to city life. Alexandra, despite its problems and flaws, gave the lie to that argument. Its population was well adapted to city life and politically conscious.

In that first year, I learned more about poverty than I did in all my childhood days in Qunu. Many days I walked the six miles to town in the morning and back in the evening in order to save the bus fare. I often went days without more than a mouthful of food and without a change of clothing. Mr Sidelsky once gave me an old suit of his and, assisted by considerable stitching and patching, I wore that suit every day for almost five years. In the end, there were more patches than suit. There is little to be said in favour of poverty, but it was often an incubator of true friendship.

My landlord, Mr Xhoma, was not wealthy, but he was a kind of philanthropist. Every Sunday, he and his wife gave me lunch, and those steaming plates of pork and vegetables

were often my only hot meal of the week. No matter where I was or what I was doing, I would never fail to be at the Xhomas' on Sunday. For the rest of the week I would sustain myself on bread, and sometimes the secretaries at the firm would bring me some food.

I gradually adjusted to township life and began to develop a sense of inner strength, a belief that I could do well outside the world in which I had grown up. I slowly discovered that I did not have to depend on my royal connections or the support of family in order to advance, and I forged relationships with people who did not know or care about my link to the Thembu royal house. I had my own home, humble though it was, and I was developing the confidence and self-reliance necessary to stand on my own two feet.

At the end of 1941 I received word that the regent was visiting Johannesburg and wanted to see me. I was nervous, but knew that I was obliged to see him and indeed wanted to do so. The regent seemed greatly changed. He never once mentioned the fact that I had run away, Fort Hare, or the arranged marriage that was not to be. He was courteous and solicitous, questioning me in a fatherly way about my studies and future plans. He did not try to dissuade me from my course, and I was grateful for this implicit acknowledgement that I was no longer his charge.

While the regent seemed satisfied with me, he was vexed with Justice, who he said must return to Mqhekezweni. Justice had formed a liaison with a young woman, and I knew he had no intention of going home.

Justice and I learned of his father's death in the winter of 1942. He had seemed weary when last I saw him and his death did not come as a great surprise. We read of the death in the newspaper because the telegram that had been sent to Justice had gone astray. We hastened down to the Transkei, arriving the day after the funeral.

I spent nearly a week in Mqhekezweni after the funeral and it was a time of retrospection and rediscovery. I realized that my own outlook and world views had evolved. I was no longer attracted by a career in the civil service, or being an interpreter in the Native Affairs Department. I no longer saw my future bound up with Thembuland and the Transkei. My life in Johannesburg, my exposure to men like Gaur Radebe and my experiences at the law firm had radically altered my beliefs.

I still felt an inner conflict between my head and my heart. My heart told me that I was a Thembu, that I had been raised and sent to school so that I could play a special role in perpetuating the kingship. Had I no obligations to the dead? To my father, who had put me in the care of the regent? To the regent himself, who had cared for me like a father? But my head told me that it was the right of every man to plan his own future as he pleased and choose his role in life. Was I not permitted to make my own choices?

Justice's circumstances were different from my own, and after the regent's death he had important new responsibilities thrust upon him. He was to succeed the regent as chief and had decided to remain in Mqhekezweni and take up his birthright. I had to return to Johannesburg, and could not even stay to attend his installation. In my language there is a saying: '*Ndiwelimilambo enamagama*' ('I have crossed famous rivers'). It means that one has travelled a great distance, that one has had wide experience and gained some wisdom from it. I thought of this as I returned to Johannesburg alone. I had, since 1934, crossed many important rivers on my way to Johannesburg. But I had many rivers yet to cross.

At the end of 1942 I passed the final examination for my BA degree. I had now achieved the rank I once considered so exalted. I was proud, but I also knew that the degree itself was neither a talisman nor a passport to easy success.

At the firm, I had become closer to Gaur, much to Mr Sidelsky's exasperation. Education, Gaur argued, was essential to our advancement, but he pointed out that no people or nation had ever freed itself through education alone. Gaur believed in finding solutions rather than in spouting theory. For Africans, he asserted, the engine of change was the African National Congress; its policies were the best way to pursue power in South Africa. He stressed the ANC's long history of advocating change, noting that it was the oldest national African organization in the country, having been founded in 1912. Its constitution denounced racialism, its presidents had been from different tribal groups, and it preached the goal of Africans as full citizens of South Africa.

I went along with Gaur to meetings of both the Township Advisory Board and the

Alexandra's atmosphere was alive, its spirit adventurous, its people resourceful. Although the township did boast some handsome buildings, it could fairly be described as a slum, living testimony to the neglect of the authorities. The roads were unpaved and dirty, and filled with hungry, undernourished children scampering around half-naked. The air was thick with the smoke from coal fires in tin braziers and stoves. A single water tap served several houses. Pools of stinking, stagnant water full of maggots collected by the side of the road.

ANC. I went as an observer, not a participant, for I do not think I ever spoke. I wanted to understand the issues under discussion, evaluate the arguments, see the calibre of the men involved. The Advisory Board meetings were perfunctory and bureaucratic, but the ANC meetings were lively with debate and discussion about Parliament, the pass laws, rents, bus fares – any subject under the sun that affected Africans.

In August 1943 I marched with Gaur and ten thousand others in support of the Alexandra bus boycott, a protest against the raising of fares from four pence to five. Gaur was one of the leaders, and I watched him in action. This campaign had a great effect on me. In a small way, I had departed from my role as an observer and become a participant. I found that to march with one's people was exhilarating and inspiring. But I was also impressed by the boycott's effectiveness: after nine days, during which the buses ran empty, the company reinstated the fare to four pence.

As far as my profession was concerned, it was Gaur who did more than offer advice. One day in early 1943, when I had been at the firm for less than two years, he took me aside and said, 'My boy, as long as I am here at the firm, they will never article you, whether or not you have a degree.' I was startled, and told Gaur that it could not be true, as he was not even training to be a lawyer. 'That does not make a difference, Nelson,' he continued. 'They will say, "We have Gaur, he can speak law to our people, why do we need someone else? Gaur is already bringing in clients to the firm." But they will not tell you this to your face; they will just postpone and delay. It is important to the future of our struggle in this country for you to become a lawyer, and so I am going to leave the firm and start my own estate agency. When I am gone, they will have no choice but to article you.'

In August 1943 I marched with ten thousand others in support of the Alexandra bus boycott, a protest against the raising of fares.

I pleaded with him not to resign, but he was immovable. Within a few days, he handed Mr Sidelsky his resignation, and Mr Sidelsky eventually articled me as promised. I cannot say whether Gaur's absence had anything to do with it, but his resignation was another example of his generosity.

Early in 1943, after passing my examination through UNISA, I returned to Fort Hare for my graduation. Before leaving for the university, I decided to treat myself to a proper suit. In order to do so, I had to borrow the money from Walter Sisulu. After the graduation I spent a few days with Daliwonga (K. D.'s clan name, which is what I called him), at his home in Qamata. Daliwonga had already chosen the path of traditional leadership and while I was staying with him he pressed me to return to Umtata after qualifying as an attorney. 'Why do you stay in Johannesburg?' he said. 'You are needed more here.'

It was a fair point: there were certainly more professional Africans in the Transvaal than in the Transkei. But in my heart I knew I was moving towards a different commitment.

At Wits, many white students went out of their way to make me feel welcome. During my first term I met Joe Slovo (below) and his future wife, Ruth First. Joe had one of the sharpest, most incisive minds I have ever encountered. He was an ardent communist, and was known for his high-spirited parties. Ruth had an outgoing personality and was a gifted writer. Both were the children of Jewish immigrants to South Africa.

Right: Walking to work during the bus boycott.

Through my friendship with Gaur and Walter, I was beginning to see that my duty was to my people as a whole, not just to a particular section or branch. I felt that all the currents in my life were taking me away from the Transkei and towards what seemed like the centre, a place where regional and ethnic loyalties gave way to a common purpose. I found myself being drawn into the world of politics because I was not content with my old beliefs.

In Johannesburg, I moved in circles where common sense and practical experience were more important than high academic qualifications. Even as I was receiving my degree, I realized that hardly anything I had learned at university seemed relevant in my new environment. At the university, teachers had shied away from topics like racial oppression, lack of opportunities for Africans and the nest of laws and regulations that subjugate the black man. But in my life in Johannesburg, I confronted these things every day. No one had ever suggested to me how to go about removing the evils of racial prejudice, and I had to learn by trial and error.

When I returned to Johannesburg at the beginning of 1943 I enrolled at the University of the Witwatersrand for a bachelor of law degree. While working at the law firm brought me into regular contact with whites for the first time, the university introduced me to a group of whites of my own age. This was as new to them as it was to me, for I was the only African student in the law faculty.

Despite the university's liberal values, I never felt entirely comfortable there. Always to be the only African, except for menial workers, to be regarded at best as a curiosity and at worst as an interloper, is not a congenial experience. My manner was always guarded, and I met both generosity and animosity. Although I was to discover a core of sympathetic whites who became friends and later colleagues, most of the whites at Wits were not liberal or colour-blind.

Our law professor, Mr Hahlo, was a strict, cerebral sort, who did not tolerate much independence on the part of his students. He held a curious view of the law when it came to women and Africans: neither group, he said, was meant to be lawyers. His view was that law was a social science and that women and Africans were not disciplined enough to master its intricacies. He once told me that I should not be at Wits but studying for my degree through UNISA. Although I disagreed with his views, I did little to disprove them. My performance as a law student was dismal.

Wits opened a new world to me, a world of ideas and political beliefs and debates, a world where people were passionate about politics. I was among white and Indian intellectuals of my own generation, young men who would form the vanguard of the most important political movements of the next few years. I discovered for the first time people of my own age firmly aligned with the liberation struggle, who were prepared, despite their relative privilege, to sacrifice themselves for the cause of the oppressed.

STOP MALAN TERROR:
PROTEST NOW!
WITH SWART'S GESTAPO BILLS—
NO CONCENTRATION CAMPS
NO MARTIAL LAW
★ STOP POLICE RAIDS
● LIVING WAGES: LOWER PRICES
★ FREE SPEECH & ASSEMBLY
● DOWN WITH APARTHEID

Birth of a Freedom Fighter

I cannot pinpoint a moment when I became politicized, when I knew that I would spend my life in the liberation struggle. I had no epiphany, no singular revelation, no moment of truth, but a steady accumulation of a thousand slights, and a thousand indignities produced in me an anger, a desire to fight the system that imprisoned my people.

One night in 1943 I met at Walter Sisulu's house Anton Lembede and A.P. Mda. From the moment I heard Lembede speak, I knew I was seeing a magnetic personality who thought in original and often startling ways. He was then one of a handful of African lawyers in the whole of South Africa and was the legal partner of Dr Pixley ka Seme, one of the founders of the ANC.

Lembede said that Africa was a black man's continent, and it was up to Africans to reassert themselves and reclaim what was rightfully theirs. He hated the idea of the black inferiority complex and castigated what he called the worship and idolization of the West and its ideas. He believed blacks had to improve their own self-image before they could initiate successful mass action.

Lembede declared that a new spirit was stirring among the people, that ethnic differences were melting away, that young men and women thought of themselves as Africans first and foremost, not as Xhosas or Ndebeles or Tswanas.

Lembede's views struck a chord in me. I, too, had been susceptible to paternalistic British colonialism and the appeal of being perceived by whites as 'cultured' and 'progressive' and 'civilized'. Like Lembede, I came to see the antidote as militant African nationalism.

Within weeks of coming to power in 1948, Malan began to implement his pernicious programme. The Nationalist government announced their intention to curb the trade union movement and do away with the limited franchises of the Indian, Coloured and African peoples. The Separate Representation of Voters Bill eventually robbed the Coloureds of their representation in Parliament. The Prohibition of Mixed Marriages Act was introduced in 1949 and was followed by the Immorality Act, making sexual relations between white and nonwhite illegal.

CITY OF DURBAN

UNDER SECTION 37 OF THE DURBAN BEACH BY-LAWS, THIS BATHING AREA IS RESERVED FOR THE SOLE USE OF MEMBERS OF THE WHITE RACE GROUP.

STAD DURBAN

HIERDIE GEBIED IS, INGEVOLGE ARTIKEL 37 VAN DIE DURBANSE STRANDVERORDENINGE UITGEHOU VIR DIE UITSLUITLIKE GEBRUIK VAN LEDE VAN DIE BLANKE RASSEGROEP.

The Population and Registration Act labelled all South Africans by race, making colour the single most important arbiter of an individual. Malan introduced the Group Areas Act – which he described as 'the very essence of apartheid' – requiring separate urban areas for each racial group.

Walter's house in Orlando was my home from home. The house was always full and there was a perpetual discussion going on about politics. It was there that I met Evelyn Mase, my first wife. She was a quiet, pretty girl who did not seem overawed by the comings and goings at the Sisulus'. She was training as a nurse at the Johannesburg non-European General Hospital.

Other young men were thinking along the same lines and we would all meet to discuss these ideas. In addition to Lembede and Mda, these men included Walter Sisulu; Oliver Tambo; Dr Lionel Majombozi; Victor Mbobo, my former teacher at Healdtown; William Nkomo, a medical student who was a member of the CP; Jordan Ngubane, a journalist from Natal who worked for *Inkundl*a as well as *Bantu World*, the largest selling African newspaper, David Bopape, secretary of the ANC in the Transvaal and a member of the Communist Party and many others. Many felt, perhaps unfairly, that the ANC as a whole had become the preserve of a tired, unmilitant, privileged African elite more concerned with protecting their own rights than those of the masses. The general consensus was that some action must be taken, and Dr Majombozi proposed forming a Youth League as a way of lighting a fire under the leadership of the ANC.

The actual formation of the Youth League took place on Easter Sunday 1944 at the Bantu Men's Social Centre in Eloff Street. There were about a hundred men there, some coming from as far away as Pretoria. Jordan Ngubane, A.P. Mda and William Nkomo all spoke, and emphasized the emerging spirit of African nationalism. Branches were soon established in all the provinces.

The basic policy of the league did not differ from the ANC's first constitution in 1912. But we were reaffirming and underscoring those original concerns, many of which had gone by the wayside. African nationalism was our battle cry, and our creed was the creation of one nation out of many tribes, the overthrow of white supremacy, and the establishment of a truly democratic form of government.

We were extremely wary of communism. Lembede and many others, including myself, considered a 'foreign' ideology unsuited to the African situation. Lembede felt that the Communist Party was dominated by whites, which undermined African self-confidence and initiative.

I asked Evelyn out very soon after our first meeting. Within a few months I had asked her to marry me, and she accepted.

The primary purpose of the Youth League was to give direction to the ANC in its quest for political freedom. Although I agreed with this, I was nervous about joining the league and still had doubts about the extent of my political commitment. I was then working full-time and studying part-time, and had little time outside those two activities. I also possessed a certain insecurity, feeling politically backward compared to Walter, Lembede and Mda.

In 1946 a number of critical events occurred that shaped my political development and the directions of the struggle. The mineworkers' strike, in which 70,000 African miners along the Reef went on strike, affected me greatly. The African Mine Workers' Union (AMWU) had been created in the early 1940s. There were as many as 400,000 African miners working on the Reef, most of them making no more than two shillings a day. The union leadership had repeatedly pressed the Chamber of Mines for a minimum wage of ten shillings a day, as well as family housing and two weeks' paid leave.

In the end, the state prevailed: the strike was suppressed and the union crushed. The strike was the beginning of my close relationship with J. B. Marks, a long-time member of the ANC and the Communist Party, and president of the African Mine Workers' Union. I visited him often, and we discussed my opposition to communism at great length. I had these same discussions with Moses Kotane and Yusuf Dadoo, both of whom believed, like Marks, that communism had to be adapted to the African situation. Other communist members of the ANC condemned me and the other Youth Leaguers for our objections, but Marks, Kotane and Dadoo never did.

After the strike, fifty-two men, including Kotane and Marks, and many other communists, were arrested and prosecuted, first for incitement, then for sedition. It was a political trial, an effort by the state to show that it was not soft on the Red Menace.

That same year, another event forced me to recast my whole approach to political work. In 1946 the Smuts government passed the Asiatic Land Tenure Act, which curtailed the free movement of Indians, circumscribed the areas where Indians could reside and trade, and severely restricted their right to buy property. This law was a grave insult to the Indian community and anticipated the Group Areas Act, which would eventually circumscribe the freedom of all South Africans of colour.

The campaign of passive resistance to oppose the measures was launched. The participation of other groups was not encouraged, but Dr Xuma and other African leaders

Led by Dr Dadoo and Dr G.M. Naicker, president of the Natal Indian Congress, the Indian community conducted an impressive mass campaign against the Asiatic Land Tenure Act. Mass rallies were held; land reserved for whites was occupied and picketed. No fewer than 2,000 volunteers went to jail, and Dr Dadoo and Dr Naicker were sentenced to six months hard labour.

spoke at several meetings, and gave full moral support to the struggle of the Indian people. The government crippled the rebellion with harsh laws and intimidation, but we in the Youth League and the ANC had witnessed the Indian people register an extraordinary protest against colour oppression in a way that Africans and the ANC had not.

Ismail Meer and J.N. Singh suspended their studies, said good-bye to their families and went to prison. Ahmed Kathrada, who was still a high-school student, did the same thing. I often visited the home of Amina Pahad for lunch, and then, suddenly, this charming woman put aside her apron and went to jail for her beliefs. If I had once questioned the willingness of the Indian community to protest against oppression, I no longer could.

The Indian campaign became a model for the type of protest that we in the Youth League were calling for. It instilled a spirit of defiance and radicalism among the people, broke the fear of prison, and boosted the popularity and influence of the NIC and TIC.

**Thembi was a solid, happy little boy who most people said resembled his mother more than his father.
I had now produced an heir, though I had little as yet to bequeath to him. But I had perpetuated the Mandela name and the Madiba clan, which is one of the basic responsibilities of a Xhosa male. When he was small, I delighted in playing with Thembi, bathing him and feeding him, and putting him to bed with a story.**

Dr Xuma, president of the ANC, speaks out against the proposals of the Group Areas Act in Drum.

Early in 1946, Evelyn and I moved to a two-room municipal house of our own in Orlando East and thereafter to a slightly larger house at No. 8115 Orlando West which would later became part of Greater Soweto. The house was identical to hundreds of others built on postage-stamp-size plots on dirt roads. It had the same standard tin roof, the same cement floor, a narrow kitchen, and a bucket toilet at the back. We used paraffin lamps as the homes were not yet electrified. The bedroom was so small that a double bed took up almost the entire floor space. These houses were built by the municipal authorities for workers who needed to be near town. To relieve the monotony, some people planted small gardens or painted their doors in bright colours. It was my first true home of my own and I was mightily proud. A man is not a man until he has a house of his own. I did not know then that it would be the only residence that would be entirely mine for many, many years. The state had allocated the house to us because we were no longer just two, but three. That year our first son, Madiba Thembekile, was born. He was given my clan name of Madiba, but was known by the nickname Thembi.

In 1947 I was elected to the Executive Committee of the Transvaal ANC and served under C.S. Ramohanoe, president of the Transvaal region. This was my first position in the ANC proper, and it represented a milestone in my commitment to the organization. From then on, I came to identify myself with the Congress as a whole; I was now bound heart and soul. Ramohanoe was a staunch nationalist and a skilful organizer who was able to balance divergent views and come forward with a suitable compromise. While Ramohanoe was unsympathetic to the communists, he worked well with them. He believed that the ANC was a national organization that should welcome all those who supported our cause.

Africans could not vote, but that did not mean that we did not care who won elections. In the white general election of 1948, the ruling United Party, led by General Smuts, opposed the revived National Party. While Smuts had enlisted South Africa on the side of the Allies in the Second World War, the National Party refused to support Great

BLACK SPOTS or WHITE SPOTS ?

by Dr. A. B. Xuma

Johannesburg City Council Plans to Move African Areas Out of Town

TO UNDERSTAND AND APPRECIATE THE IMPLI-CATIONS of the proposal (agreed to between the Government on the one hand and the City Council of Johannesburg on the other) to remove Sophiatown, Martindale and Newclare, the so-called "black spots" on the Western areas of Johannesburg, it is necessary to discuss it not in isolation but against the general background of the housing of Africans in Johannesburg of which it is an integral and inseparable part.

The townships of Sophiatown, Martindale and Newclare, comprising an area of roughly 210 morgen, which are the only townships in the Johannesburg area where an African may buy property and have freehold title to it, were established in 1903, 1905 and 1912 respectively. It is worthy to note that there has been no more freehold areas where Africans may buy and own property ever since. In fact, in recent years even in these areas the African is restricted to buy from other Africans.

THE AUTHOR, DR. A. B. XUMA, is chairman of the Western Areas Anti-Expropriation and Proper Housing Committee. A former President of the African National Congress, he is a well-known public figure and a medical practitioner. He lives in Sophiatown.

He may buy from a non-African only if he obtains the Governor-General's consent to the transaction. Africans may not buy a home or land anywhere else in Johannesburg.

The proposal to remove these areas, therefore, is a calculated attempt to undermine, if not destroy, freehold ownership of land by Africans.

ONCE MILES FROM TOWN

IT is well to remember that when these townships were laid out at the beginning of the century, they were miles away from the town with no transport facilities or communications with Johannesburg. Johannesburg itself was little more than a mining camp. Added to the problem of transport and long distance from the town, these townships half-encircled a sewage farm where the Municipal Western Native Location now stands. It is reasonable to believe, therefore, that they were generally considered not only unsuitable for human habitation but also without economic value. They were "out of sight and out of mind" where, to adopt a common South African cliche, "Natives could develop along their own lines."

The isolated position was to be only temporary. Gold mining, with its ancillary industries, as well as secondary industries, developed and the white population of Johannesburg grew with industrial demands. Johannesburg expanded westward until the European townships encroached upon and encircled these areas, as we find them today to raise the present political hue and cry of "black spots" in the midst of white areas.

VOTE-CATCHING SLOGAN

It is advisable to mention, in passing, that all this agitation for the removal of these townships does not come from the ordinary residents of the surrounding white areas who are occupied full time on bread-winning activities but emanates from politicians, Ministers of the Crown, Members of Parliament, Provincial and City councillors or candidates.

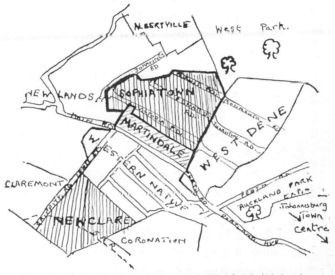

Map of the Western Areas: The shaded areas are the "Black Spots" which the Johannesburg City Council plan to move further out of the city. Note how Western Native Township, which is in the middle of the area, is now scheduled to remain where it is; the coloured location of Albertville is also now excluded from the scheme. Coronation is another coloured township, and Claremont and Westdene, both of which border on the "Black Spots," are European districts. The main Johannesburg-Roodepoort Road passes through the middle of the "Black Spots" Area.

Where Black meets White: A Street Corner in the Western Areas, where a White Spot (right) adjoins a Black Spot (left).

General Smuts, leader of the ruling United Party, during the 1948 election campaign. A Nationalist victory was a shock. The United Party and General Smuts had beaten the Nazis; surely they would defeat the National Party.

Britain and publicly sympathized with Nazi Germany. The Nationalists were led by Dr Daniel Malan, a former minister of the Dutch Reformed Church and a newspaper editor.

Malan's platform was known as apartheid. *Apartheid* was a new term but an old idea. It literally means 'apartness', and it represented the codification in one oppressive system of all the laws and regulations that had kept Africans in an inferior position to whites for centuries. The often haphazard segregation of the past three hundred years was to be consolidated into a monolithic system that was diabolical in its detail, inescapable in its reach and overwhelming in its power. The policy was supported by the Dutch Reformed Church, which furnished apartheid with its religious underpinnings by suggesting that Afrikaners were God's chosen people and that blacks were a subservient species.

A Nationalist victory was a shock. I was stunned and dismayed. For the first time in South African history, an exclusively Afrikaner party led the government. 'South Africa belongs to us once more,' Malan proclaimed in his victory speech.

In response to this new and much more powerful threat from the state, the ANC embarked on an effort to turn itself into a truly mass organization. At the 1949 ANC annual conference in Bloemfontein, the organization adopted the league's Programme of Action, which called for boycotts, strikes, stay-at-homes, passive resistance, protest demonstrations and other forms of mass action. This was a radical change: the ANC's policy had always been to keep its activities within the law. We in the Youth League had seen the failure of legal and constitutional means to strike at racial oppression; now the entire organization was set to enter a more activist stage.

These changes did not come without internal upheaval. A few weeks before the conference, Walter Sisulu, Oliver Tambo, A.P. Mda and I met Dr Xuma privately at his home in Sophiatown. We explained that we thought the time had come for mass action along the lines of Gandhi's non-violent protests in India and the 1946 passive resistance campaign, asserting that the ANC had become too docile in the face of oppression. Dr Xuma was adamantly opposed, claiming that such strategies were premature and would merely give the government an excuse to crush the ANC.

A newspaper cartoon highlights the fact that the National Party publicly sympathized with Nazi Germany.

We gave Dr Xuma an ultimatum: we would support him for re-election to the presidency of the ANC provided he supported our proposed Programme of Action. As an alternative candidate, we sponsored Dr J.S. Moroka. Dr Moroka was an unlikely choice. He was a member of the All-African Convention (AAC) which was dominated by Trotskyite elements. When he agreed to stand against Dr Xuma, the Youth League then enrolled him as a member of the ANC. He was not very knowledgeable about the ANC, but he was respectable, and amenable to our programme. Dr Xuma was defeated and Dr Moroka became

president-general of the ANC. Walter Sisulu was elected the new secretary-general, and
Oliver Tambo was elected to the National Executive.

The Programme of Action approved at the annual conference called for the pursuit of
political rights through the use of boycotts, strikes, civil disobedience and non-
cooperation. In addition, it called for a national day of work stoppage in protest against the
racist and reactionary policies of the government. This was a departure from the days of
decorous protest, and many of the old stalwarts of the ANC were to fade away in this new
era of greater militancy. Youth League members had graduated to the senior organization.
We had now guided the ANC to a more radical and revolutionary path.

The spirit of mass action surged, but I remained sceptical of any action undertaken
with the communists and Indians. The 'Defend Free Speech Convention' in March 1950
organized by the Transvaal ANC, the Transvaal Indian Congress, the African People's
Organization and the District Committee of the Communist Party drew ten thousand

The Group Areas Act was the foundation of residential apartheid. Under its regulations, each racial group could own land, occupy premises and trade only in its own separate area. The Act initiated the era of forced removals, when African communities, towns and villages in newly designated white urban areas were violently relocated.

NATIONAL DAY OF PROTEST

MONDAY, 26TH JUNE, 1950
Begins the all out struggle for Freedom.

Dr. J. S. Moroka, President-General of the African National Congress, supported by Leaders of the South African South African Indian Congress, and African Peoples' Organisation calls upon all South Africans to REFRAIN FROM GOING TO WORK ON THIS DAY.

•

- DEFEAT THE SUPPRESSION OF COMMUNISM AND THE GROUP AREAS BILLS WHICH WILL TURN OUR COUNTRY INTO A POLICE STATE.
- DON'T ALLOW MALAN GOVERNMENT'S OPPRESSIVE FASCIST MEASURES TO CRUSH OUR LIVES & LIBERTIES !
- FIGHT FOR FREEDOM — PASS LAWS AND POLICE RAIDS MUST GO! LAND, VOTES AND DECENT WAGES FOR ALL!

'Tis better to sacrifice all in the struggle for Freedom rather than live as slaves.

African, Coloured, Indian and European Democrats—FREEDOM NOT SERFDOM!

At the top of the list for removal was Sophiatown (right), a vibrant community of more than fifty thousand people, which was one of the oldest black settlements in Johannesburg.

people to Johannesburg's Market Square. Dr Moroka, without consulting the Executive, agreed to preside over the convention. The convention was a success, yet I remained wary, as the prime mover behind it was the party.

At the instigation of the Communist Party and the Indian Congress, the convention passed a resolution for a one-day general strike, known as Freedom Day, on 1 May, calling for the abolition of the pass laws and all discriminatory legislation. Although I supported these objectives, I believed that the communists were trying to steal the thunder from the ANC's National Day of Protest. I opposed the May Day strike on the grounds that the ANC had not originated the campaign, believing that we should concentrate on our own campaign.

The Freedom Day strike went ahead without official ANC support. Despite protest and criticism, the Nationalist government responded by introducing the notorious Suppression of Communism Act, and the ANC called an emergency conference in Johannesburg. While the act outlawed the Communist Party of South Africa and made it a crime, punishable by a maximum of ten years' imprisonment, to be a member of the party or to further the aims of communism, essentially, it permitted the government to outlaw any organization and to restrict any individual opposed to its policies.

Clearly, the repression of any one liberation group was repression of all liberation groups. At the meeting to discuss these measures Oliver uttered prophetic words: 'Today it is the Communist Party. Tomorrow it will be our trade unions, our Indian Congress, our APO, our African National Congress.' Supported by the SAIC and the APO, the ANC resolved to stage a National Day of Protest on 26 June 1950.

Earlier that year I had been co-opted onto the National Executive Committee of the ANC. Now, as a member of the National Executive, I was playing in the first team with the most senior people in the ANC.

Mass action was perilous in South Africa, where it was a criminal offence for an African to strike, and where the rights of free speech and movement were unmercifully curtailed. By striking, an African worker stood to lose not only his job but his right to stay in the area in which he was living. In my experience, a political strike is always riskier than an economic one. A strike based on a political grievance rather than on clear-cut issues such as higher wages or shorter hours is a more precarious form of protest and demands particularly efficient organization. The Day of Protest was a political rather than an economic strike.

In preparation for 26 June, Walter travelled around the country consulting local leaders. In his absence, I took charge of the bustling ANC office, the hub of a complicated national action.

The Day of Protest was the ANC's first attempt to hold a political strike on a national scale, and it was a moderate success. In the cities, the majority of workers stayed at home

and black businesses did not open. The Day of Protest boosted our morale, made us realize our strength and sent a warning to the Malan government that we would not remain passive in the face of apartheid. 26 June has since become a landmark day in the freedom struggle, and within the liberation movement it is observed as Freedom Day.

If we had any hopes or illusions about the National Party before they came into office, we were disabused of them quickly. Their threat to put the kaffir in his place was not an idle one. Apart from the Suppression of Communism Act, two laws passed in 1950 formed the cornerstones of apartheid: the Population Registration Act and the Group Areas Act. If it had not already been so, race became the *sine qua non* of South African society. The arbitrary and meaningless tests to decide black from Coloured or Coloured from white often resulted in tragic cases where members of the same family were classified differently, all depending on whether one child had a lighter or darker complexion.

The following year, the government passed two more laws that directly attacked the rights of Coloureds and Africans. The Separate Representation of Voters Act aimed to transfer Coloureds to a separate voters' roll in the Cape, thereby diluting the franchise rights that they had enjoyed for more than a century. The Bantu Authorities Act abolished the Natives' Representative Council, the one indirect forum of national representation for Africans, and replaced it with a hierarchical system of tribal chiefs appointed by the government.

The Coloured people rallied against the Separate Representation of Voters Act, organizing a tremendous demonstration in Cape Town in March 1951 and a strike in April that kept shops closed and schoolchildren at home. It was in the context of this spirit of activism by Indians, Coloureds and Africans that Walter Sisulu first broached the idea to a small group of us of a national civil disobedience campaign. He outlined a plan under which selected volunteers from all groups would deliberately invite imprisonment by defying certain laws.

The idea immediately appealed to me, as it did to the others, but I urged that the campaign should be exclusively African. The average African, I said, was still cautious about joint action with Indians and Coloureds. While I had made progress in terms of my opposition to communism, I still feared the influence of Indians. In addition, many of our grassroots African supporters saw Indians as exploiters of black labour in their role as shopkeepers and merchants.

Walter vehemently disagreed, suggesting that the Indians, Coloureds and Africans were inextricably bound together. The issue was taken up at a meeting of the National Executive Committee and my view was voted down, even by those who were considered staunch African nationalists.

The ANC conference endorsed a resolution calling upon the government to repeal the Suppression of Communism Act, the Group Areas Act, the Separate Representation of Voters Act, the Bantu Authorities Act, the pass laws and stock limitation laws by 29 February 1952. The law was intended to reduce overgrazing by cattle, but its impact would

All across the country, those who defied on 26 June did so with courage, enthusiasm and a sense of history. These women are emerging from prison after being jailed for defying the unjust laws.

be to further curtail land for Africans. The council resolved that the ANC would hold demonstrations on 6 April 1952 as a prelude to the launching of the Campaign for the Defiance of Unjust Laws.

The ANC wrote to the prime minister advising him of these resolutions and the deadline for repealing the laws. It noted that the ANC had exhausted every constitutional means at our disposal to achieve our legitimate rights, and that we demanded the repeal of the six 'unjust laws' by 29 February 1952, or else we would take extra-constitutional action. Malan's reply asserted that whites had an inherent right to take measures to preserve their own identity as a separate community, and ended with the threat that if we pursued our actions the government would not hesitate to make full use of its machinery to quell any disturbances.

We regarded Malan's curt dismissal of our demands as a declaration of war. We now had no alternative but to resort to civil disobedience. On 6 April preliminary demonstrations took place in Johannesburg, Pretoria, Port Elizabeth, Durban and Cape Town. While Dr Moroka addressed a crowd at Freedom Square in Johannesburg, I spoke to a group of potential volunteers at the Garment Workers' Union. I explained to a group of several hundred Africans, Indians and Coloureds that volunteering was a difficult and even dangerous duty as the authorities would seek to intimidate, imprison and perhaps attack the volunteers. No matter what the authorities did, they must respond to violence with non-violence; discipline must be maintained at all costs.

On 31 May the Executives of the ANC and the SAIC announced that the Defiance Campaign would begin on 26 June, the anniversary of the first National Day of Protest. They also created a National Action Committee to direct the campaign and a National Volunteer Board to recruit and train volunteers. I was appointed national volunteer-in-chief of the campaign and chairman of both the Action Committee and the Volunteer Board.

The joint planning council agreed upon an open-ended programme of non-cooperation and non-violence. Two stages of defiance were proposed. In the first stage, a small number of well-trained volunteers would break selected laws in a handful of urban areas. They would enter proscribed areas without permits, use Whites Only facilities such as toilets, Whites Only railway compartments, waiting rooms and post office entrances. They would deliberately remain in town after curfew. Each batch of defiers would have a leader who would inform the police in advance of the act of disobedience so that the arrests could take place with a minimum of disturbance. The second stage was envisioned as mass defiance, accompanied by strikes and industrial actions across the country.

Prior to the inauguration of the Defiance Campaign, a rally, called the Day of the

Consultation with Dr Moroka, president of the ANC (left), and Dr Dadoo during the Defiance Campaign.

Volunteers, was held in Durban on 22 June. Chief Luthuli, president of the Natal ANC, and Dr Naicker, president of the Natal Indian Congress, both spoke and committed themselves to the campaign. I was the main speaker. About ten thousand people were in attendance, and I told the crowd that the Defiance Campaign would be the most powerful action ever undertaken by the oppressed masses in South Africa and that they would make history and focus the attention of the world on the racist policies of South Africa. I emphasized that unity among the black people – Africans, Coloureds and Indians – in South Africa had at last become a reality.

On that first day of the Defiance Campaign more than 250 volunteers around the country violated various unjust laws and were imprisoned. It was an auspicious beginning. Our troops were orderly, disciplined, and confident.

Over the next five months, 8,500 people took part in the campaign. Doctors, factory workers, lawyers, teachers, students, ministers, defied and went to jail. The campaign spread throughout the Witwatersrand, to Durban and to Port Elizabeth, East London and Cape Town, and smaller towns in the eastern and western Cape. Resistance was beginning to percolate even in the rural areas. For the most part, the offences were minor, and the penalties ranged from no more than a few nights in jail to a few weeks, with the option of a fine which rarely exceeded £10. The campaign received an enormous amount of publicity and the membership of the ANC shot up from some 20,000 to 100,000, with the most spectacular increase occurring in the eastern Cape, which contributed half of all new members.

The government saw the campaign as a threat to its security and its policy of apartheid. They regarded civil disobedience as a crime, and were perturbed by the growing partnership between Africans and Indians. Apartheid was designed to divide racial groups, and we showed that different groups could work together. The prospect of a united front between Africans and Indians, between moderates and radicals, greatly worried them. The Nationalists insisted that the campaign was instigated by communist agitators and responded in 1953 with the Public Safety Act, which empowered the government to declare martial law and to detain people without trial, and the Criminal Laws Amendment Act, which authorized corporal punishment for defiers.

In May, during the middle of the Defiance Campaign, J. B. Marks was banned under the 1950 Suppression of Communism Act for 'furthering the aims of communism'. Banning was a legal order by the government, and generally entailed forced resignation from indicated organizations, and restriction from attending gatherings of any kind. It was a kind of walking imprisonment. To violate or ignore a banning order was to invite imprisonment.

At the Transvaal conference that year in October, my name was proposed to replace the banned J. B. Marks. I was the national president of the Youth League, and the favourite for Marks's position. Although my candidacy did not go unopposed I won the election with an overwhelming majority.

On 30 July 1952, at the height of the Defiance Campaign, I was at work at my then law firm of H.M. Basner when the police arrived with a warrant for my arrest. The charge was violation of the Suppression of Communism Act. The state made a series of simultaneous arrests of campaign leaders in Johannesburg, Port Elizabeth and Kimberley. Earlier in the month, the police had raided homes and offices of ANC and SAIC officials all over the country and confiscated papers and documents. This type of raid was something new and set a pattern for the pervasive and illegal searches that subsequently became a regular feature of the government's behaviour.

My arrest and those of the others culminated in a trial in September in Johannesburg of twenty-one accused, including the presidents and general secretaries of the ANC, the SAIC, the ANC Youth League and the Transvaal Indian Congress. Among the twenty-one on trial in Johannesburg were Dr Moroka, Walter Sisulu and J.B. Marks. A number of Indian leaders were arrested, including Dr Dadoo, Yusuf Cachalia and Ahmed Kathrada.

The trial should have been an occasion of resolve and solidarity, but Dr Moroka, the president-general of the ANC and the figurehead of the campaign, shocked us all by employing his own attorney.

On 2 December we were all found guilty of what Judge Rumpff defined as 'statutory communism'. According to the statutes of the Suppression of Communism Act, virtually anyone who opposed the government in any way could be defined as – and therefore convicted of being – a 'statutory communist', even without ever having been a member of the party. The judge, who was fair-minded and reasonable, said that although we had planned acts that ranged from 'open non-compliance of laws to something that equals high treason', he accepted that we had consistently advised our members 'to follow a peaceful course of action and to avoid violence in any shape or form'. We were sentenced to nine months' imprisonment with hard labour, but the sentence was suspended for two years.

We made many mistakes, but the Defiance Campaign marked a new chapter in the struggle. The six laws we singled out were not overturned; but we never had any illusion that they would be. We selected them as the most immediate burden pressing on the lives of the people, and the best way to engage the greatest number of people in the struggle.

Our membership swelled to 100,000. The ANC emerged as a truly mass-based organization with an impressive corps of experienced activists who had braved the police, the courts and the jails. The stigma usually associated with imprisonment had been removed. This was a significant achievement, for fear of prison is a tremendous hindrance to a liberation struggle. From the Defiance Campaign onward, going to prison became a badge of honour among Africans.

I felt a great sense of accomplishment and satisfaction. The campaign freed me from any lingering sense of doubt or inferiority I might still have felt; it liberated me from the feeling of being overwhelmed by the power and seeming invincibility of the white man and his institutions. I had come of age as a freedom fighter.

The Struggle Is My Life

At the ANC annual conference at the end of 1952, there was a changing of the guard. The ANC designated a new, more vigorous, president: Chief Albert Luthuli, one of a handful of ruling chiefs who were active in the ANC. As provincial president of the Transvaal, I became one of the four deputy presidents and the National Executive Committee appointed me as First Deputy President.

I was unable to attend the national conference. A few days before the conference was to begin, fifty-two leaders around the country were banned from attending any meetings or gatherings for six months. I was among those leaders, and my movements were restricted to the district of Johannesburg. My bans extended to meetings of all kinds, not only political ones. I could not, for example, attend my son's birthday party. This was part of a systematic effort by the government to silence, persecute and immobilize the leaders of those fighting apartheid.

Along with many others, I had become convinced that the government intended to declare the ANC and the SAIC illegal organizations, just as it had done with the Communist Party. I approached the National Executive with the idea that we must come up with a contingency plan for just such an eventuality. They instructed me to draw up a plan that would enable the organization to operate from underground. This strategy came to be known as the Mandela-Plan or, simply, M-Plan. It would allow an illegal organization to continue to function and enable leaders who were banned to continue to lead.

The streets of Sophiatown were narrow and unpaved, and every plot was filled with dozens of shanties huddled close together. As industry in Johannesburg grew, Sophiatown became the home of a rapidly expanding African workforce. Several families might all be crowded into a single shanty. Up to forty people could share a single water tap.

In 1951, after I had completed my articles at Witkin, Sidelsky and Eidelman, I went to work for the law firm of Terblanche & Briggish. I had investigated a number of white firms – there were, of course, no African law firms. After about one year, I joined the firm of Helman and Michel. It was a liberal firm, and one of the few that charged Africans on a reasonable scale. In addition, it prided itself on its devotion to African education, towards which it donated handsomely.

I stayed at Helman and Michel for a number of months while I was studying for my qualification exam, which would establish me as a fully-fledged attorney. When I passed the exam, I went to work as a fully-fledged attorney at the firm of H.M. Basner. Basner had been an Africans' representative in the Senate, an early member of the Communist Party, and a passionate supporter of African rights. As a lawyer, he was a defender of African leaders and trade unionists. After the experience I gained there, I felt ready to go off on my own.

In August 1952 I opened my own law office. Oliver Tambo was then working for a firm called Kovalsky and Tuch and I often visited him there during his lunch hour. Oliver and I were very good friends, and we mainly discussed ANC business during those lunch hours. He had first impressed me at Fort Hare where I noticed his thoughtful intelligence and sharp debating skills. With his cool, logical style he could demolish an opponent's argument – precisely the sort of intelligence that is useful in a courtroom. He was also a neighbour:

he came from Bizana in Pondoland, part of the Transkei, and his face bore the distinctive scars of his tribe. It seemed natural for us to practise together and I asked him to join me. A few months later, we opened our own office in downtown Johannesburg.

'Mandela and Tambo' read the brass plate on our office door in Chancellor House, a small building just across the street from the magistrates' court in central Johannesburg. From the beginning, Mandela and Tambo was besieged

At the newly opened offices of Mandela and Tambo, 1952.

Oliver Tambo (above right) in his previous office at Kovalsky and Tuch.

with clients. We were not the only African lawyers in South Africa, but we were the only firm of African lawyers. To reach our offices each morning, we had to move through a crowd of people in the corridors, on the stairs and in our small waiting room.

Africans were desperate for legal help: it was a crime to walk through a Whites Only door, a crime to ride a Whites Only bus, a crime to use a Whites Only drinking fountain, a crime to walk on a Whites Only beach, a crime to be on the streets after 11 p.m., a crime not to have a pass book and a crime to have the wrong signature in that book, a crime to be unemployed and a crime to be employed in the wrong place, a crime to live in certain places and a crime to have no place to live.

I realized quickly what Mandela and Tambo meant to ordinary Africans. It was a place

where they could come and find a sympathetic ear and a competent ally, a place where they would not be either turned away or cheated, a place where they might actually feel proud to be represented by men of their own skin colour.

Situated four miles west of Johannesburg's centre was the African township of Sophiatown, part of what was known as the Western Areas townships. The area was originally intended for whites, and a property developer actually built a number of houses there for white buyers. But because of a municipal refuse dump in the area, whites chose to live elsewhere. Reluctantly, the developer sold his houses to Africans.

In Johannesburg, the Western Areas Removal scheme meant the evacuation of Sophiatown. In 1953, the Nationalist government had purchased a tract of land called Meadowlands, thirteen miles from the city. People were to be resettled there in seven different 'ethnic groups'. The excuse given by the government was slum clearance, a smokescreen for the government policy that regarded all urban areas as white areas where Africans were temporary residents.

The government was under pressure from its supporters in the surrounding areas of

Westdene and Newlands, which were comparatively poor white areas. These working-class whites were envious of some of the fine houses owned by blacks in Sophiatown. The government wanted to control the movements of all Africans, and such control was far more difficult in freehold urban townships, where blacks could own property, and people came and went as they pleased. Though the pass system was still in effect, one did not need a special permit to enter a freehold township, as was the case with municipal locations. Africans had lived and owned property in Sophiatown for over fifty years; now the government was callously planning on relocating all Sophiatown's African residents to another black township. The removal of Sophiatown was the first major test of strength for the ANC and its allies after the Defiance Campaign.

The ANC was then holding meetings every Sunday evening in Freedom Square, in the centre of Sophiatown, to mobilise opposition to the removal. These were vibrant sessions. The meetings were addressed by leading ANC members, standholders, tenants, city councillors, and often by Father Huddleston, who ignored police warnings to confine himself to church affairs.

One Sunday evening I was scheduled to speak in Freedom Square. The crowd that night was passionate, and their emotion undoubtedly influenced mine. There were a great many young people present, and they were angry and eager for action. As usual, policemen were clustered around the perimeter, armed with both guns and pencils, the latter to take notes of who was speaking and what the speaker was saying.

I began by speaking about the increasing repressiveness of the government in the wake of the Defiance Campaign. I said the government was now scared of the might of the African people. As I spoke, I grew more and more indignant and I overstepped the line: I said that the time for passive resistance had ended, that non-violence was a useless strategy and could never overturn a white minority regime bent on retaining its power at any cost. At the end of the day, I said, violence was the only weapon that would destroy apartheid. The crowd was excited; the youth in particular were clapping and cheering. They were ready to act on what I said right then and there.

But my words that night did not come out of nowhere. I had been thinking of the future. The Nationalist government was making any legal expression of dissent or protest impossible. I saw that it would ruthlessly suppress any legitimate protest on the part of the African majority. A police state did not seem far off.

In Johannesburg, I had become a man of the city. I wore smart suits, drove an Oldsmobile and commuted daily to a downtown office. But I remained a country boy at heart, and there was nothing that lifted my spirits as much as blue skies, the open veld and green grass. In September, as my banning orders had ended, I decided to take advantage of my freedom and get some respite from the city. I took on a case in the little dorp of Villiers in the Orange Free State.

The drive to Villiers cheered me considerably, and I was labouring under a false sense

ANC meetings in Sophiatown were often addressed by Father Huddleston.

of security when I entered the small courthouse on the morning of 3 September. I found a group of policemen waiting to serve me with an order under the Suppression of Communism Act requiring me to resign from the ANC, restricting me to the Johannesburg district and prohibiting me from attending any meetings or gatherings for two years.

I was thirty-five, and these new severe bans ended a period of nearly a decade of involvement with the ANC, years that had been the time of my political awakening and growth, and my gradual commitment to the struggle that had become my life. Henceforth, all my actions and plans on behalf of the ANC and the liberation struggle would become secret and illegal. I had to return to Johannesburg immediately.

The Transvaal conference of the ANC was due to be held the following month, and I had already completed the draft of my presidential address. It was read to the conference by Andrew Kunene, a member of the Executive. In that speech, I said that the masses now had to be prepared for new forms of political struggle. The new laws and tactics of the government had made the old forms of mass protest – public meetings, press statements, stay-aways – extremely dangerous and self-destructive. Newspapers would not publish our statements and printing presses refused to print our leaflets, all for fear of prosecution under the Suppression of Communism Act. These developments required the evolution of new forms of political struggle.

Sparring with Jerry Moloi at his gym in Orlando. The gym was poorly equipped. We could not afford a ring and trained on a cement floor, which was particularly dangerous when a boxer was knocked down. We boasted a single punch-bag and a few pairs of boxing gloves. Despite the lack of equipment, the gym produced such champions as Eric (Black Material) Ntsele, bantamweight champion of South Africa, and Freddie (Tomahawk) Ngidi, the Transvaal flyweight champion, who spent his days working for me as an assistant at Mandela and Tambo

The province of the Orange Free State has always had a magical effect on me, though some of the most racist elements of the white population call the Free State their home. With its flat dusty landscape as far as the eye can see, the great blue ceiling above, the endless stretches of yellow mealie fields, scrub and bushes, the Free State's landscape gladdens my heart no matter what my mood. When I am there I feel that nothing can shut me in, that my thoughts can roam as far and wide as the horizons.

The end of the anti-removal campaign in Sophiatown, February 1955. The army and the police were relentlessly efficient. After a few weeks, our resistance collapsed. Most of our local leaders had been banned or arrested and, in the end, Sophiatown died not to the sound of gunfire but to the sound of rumbling trucks and sledgehammers. The demolition force pauses (right) before moving in.

The anti-removal campaign in Sophiatown was a long-running battle. Throughout 1954 and into 1955, rallies were held twice a week. Speaker after speaker continued to decry the government's plans. The ANC and the Ratepayers Association, under the direction of Dr Xuma, protested to the government in letters and petitions. We ran the campaign on the slogan 'Over Our Dead Bodies', a motto often shouted from the platforms and echoed by the audience.

The night before the removal, Joe Modise, one of the most dedicated of the local ANC leaders, addressed a tense meeting of youthful activists. They expected the ANC to give them an order to defy the police and the army. They were prepared to erect barricades overnight and engage the police with weapons and whatever came to hand the next day. They assumed our slogan meant what it said: that Sophiatown would be removed only over our dead bodies. But after discussions with the ANC leadership, including myself, Joe told the youth to stand down. They were angry and felt betrayed. But we believed that violence would have been a disaster.

In the hazy dawn hours of 9 February, four thousand police and army troops cordoned off the township while workers razed empty houses, and government trucks began moving families from Sophiatown to Meadowlands.

We made a variety of mistakes in the campaign and learned a number of lessons. The 'Over Our Dead Bodies' slogan caught the imagination of the people, but it led them to believe that we would fight to the death to resist the removal. In fact, the ANC was not prepared to do that at all. The lesson I took away from the campaign was that, in the end, we had no alternative to armed and violent resistance. Over and over again, we had used all the non-violent weapons in our arsenal – speeches, deputations, threats, marches, strikes, stay-aways, voluntary imprisonment – all to no avail, for whatever we did was met by an iron hand.

Until the passing of the Bantu Education Act, most Africans were educated in church and mission schools.

Since the turn of the century, Africans owed their educational opportunities primarily to the foreign churches and missions that created and sponsored schools. Under the United Party, the syllabus for African secondary schools and white secondary schools was essentially the same. The mission schools provided Africans with Western-style English-language education, which I myself received. We were limited by lesser facilities, but not by what we could read or think or dream.

In 1953 the Nationalist-dominated Parliament passed the Bantu Education Act, which sought to put apartheid's stamp on African education. The act transferred control of African education from the Department of Education to

the much loathed Native Affairs Department. Under the act, African primary and secondary schools operated by Church and mission bodies were given the choice of turning over their schools to the government or receiving gradually diminished subsidies. African teachers were not permitted to criticize the government or any school authority. Dr Hendrik Verwoerd, the minister of Bantu Education, explained that education 'must train and teach people in accordance with their opportunities in life.' His meaning was that Africans did not and would not have any opportunities; therefore, why educate them?

To the ANC, the act was a deeply sinister measure designed to retard the progress of African culture as a whole and, if enacted, permanently set back the freedom struggle of the African people.

The act and Verwoerd's crude exposition of it aroused widespread indignation from both black and white. With the exception of the Dutch Reformed Church, which supported apartheid, and the Lutheran mission, all Christian churches opposed the new measure – though the unity of the opposition extended only to condemning the policy, not resisting it.

The transfer of control to the Native Affairs Department was set to take place on 1 April 1955, and the ANC began to discuss plans for a school boycott that would begin on that date. Our secret discussions in the Executive turned on whether we should call on the people to stage a protest for a limited period or whether we should proclaim a permanent school boycott to destroy the Bantu Education Act before it could take root.

The National Executive resolved that a week-long school boycott should begin on 1 April. This was recommended at the annual conference in Durban in December 1954, but the delegates rejected the recommendation and voted for an indefinite boycott. The conference was the supreme authority, even greater than the Executive, and we found ourselves saddled with a boycott that would be almost impossible to effect. Dr Verwoerd announced that the government would permanently close all schools that were boycotted and that children who stayed away would not be readmitted.

For this boycott to work, the parents and the community would have to step in and take the place of the schools. I spoke to parents and ANC members and told them that every home, every shack, every community structure, must become a centre of learning for our children.

In Germiston, a township southeast of the city, Joshua Makue, chairman of our local branch, ran a school for eight hundred boycotting children that lasted for three years. In Port Elizabeth, Barrett Tyesi gave up a government teaching post and ran a school for boycotting children. In 1956, he presented seventy of these children for the Standard VI exams; all but three passed. In many places, improvised schools (described as 'cultural clubs' in order not to attract the attention of the authorities) taught boycotting students. The government subsequently passed a law that made it an offence punishable by fine or imprisonment to offer unauthorized education. Police harassed these clubs, but many continued to exist underground.

In the end, the community schools withered away and parents, faced with a choice between inferior education and no education at all, chose the former. My own children were at the Seventh Day Adventist school, which was private and did not depend on government subsidies.

The campaign should be judged on two levels: whether the immediate objective was achieved, and whether it politicized more people and drew them into the struggle. On the first level, the campaign clearly failed. We did not close down African schools throughout the country, neither did we rid ourselves of the Bantu Education Act. In the end we had no option but to choose between the lesser of two evils, and agree to a diminished education. But the consequences of Bantu Education came back to haunt the government in unforeseen ways. For it was Bantu Education that produced in the 1970s the angriest, most rebellious generation of black youth the country had ever seen. When these children of Bantu Education entered their late teens and early twenties, they rose with a vehemence.

Several months after Chief Luthuli was elected president of the ANC, Professor Z. K. Matthews returned to South

Demonstration against the Bantu Education Act. The boycott began on 1 April 1955 and had mixed results. It was often sporadic, disorganized and ineffectual. On the east Rand it affected some seven thousand schoolchildren. Pre-dawn marches called on parents to keep their children at home. Women picketed the schools and plucked out children who had wandered into them.

Africa armed with an idea that would reshape the liberation struggle: that the ANC draw up a Freedom Charter for the democratic South Africa of the future.

Within months a Council of the Congress of the People was created, with Chief Luthuli as chairman and Walter Sisulu and Yusuf Cachalia as joint secretaries. The Congress of the People was to create a set of principles for the foundation of a new South Africa. Suggestions for a new constitution were to come from the people themselves, and ANC leaders all across the country were authorized to seek ideas in writing from everyone in their area.

We invited some two hundred organizations – white, black, Indian and Coloured – to send representatives to a planning conference at Tongaat, near Durban, in March 1954. The National Action Council created there invited all participating organizations and their followers to send suggestions for a freedom charter. Circulars were sent out to townships and villages all across the country. Some of the flyers and leaflets were filled with the poetic idealism that characterized the planning.

Suggestions came in from sports and cultural clubs, church groups, ratepayers' associations, women's organizations, schools, trade union branches. The most commonly cited demand was for one-man-one-vote.

The Congress of the People took place at Kliptown, a multiracial village a few miles southwest of Johannesburg, on 25 and 26 June 1955. Although the overwhelming number of delegates were black, there were more than three hundred Indians, two hundred Coloureds and one hundred whites. White and African police and members of the Special Branch milled around, taking photographs and trying unsuccessfully to intimidate the delegates.

On the afternoon of the first day, the charter was read aloud, section by section, to the people in English, Sesotho and Xhosa. After each section, the crowd shouted its approval. The first day of the Congress was a success.

The second day was much like the first. Each section of the charter had been adopted by acclamation, and at 3.30 the final approval was to be voted when a brigade of police and Special Branch detectives brandishing sten guns swarmed on to the platform. One of the police took the microphone and announced that treason was suspected and that no one was to leave the gathering without police permission. The police began pushing people off the platform and confiscating documents and photographs. Another group of constables armed with rifles formed a cordon round the crowd. The people responded magnificently by loudly singing '*Nkosi Sikelel' iAfrika*'. The delegates were then allowed to leave one by one, each person interviewed by the police and his or her name taken down. As I returned to Johannesburg, I knew that this raid signalled a harsh new turn on the part of the government.

On my trip back to the Transkei, September 1955, I ate the same foods I had eaten as a boy, I walked the same fields and gazed at the same sky during the day, the same stars at night.

Though the Congress of the People had been broken up, the charter itself became a great beacon for the liberation struggle. It captured the hopes and dreams of the people and acted as a blueprint for the liberation struggle and the future of the nation.

In early September 1955, my bans expired. I had last had a holiday in 1948 and since then I had been confined to Johannesburg for two years, chained to my legal and political work. I was anxious to see my family and confer with Sabata and Daliwonga on certain problems involving the Transkei, while the ANC was eager that I confer with them on political matters.

When I turned into York Road, the main street of Umtata, I felt the rush of familiarity and fond memories one gets from coming home after a long exile. I had been away for thirteen years, and while there were no banners and fatted calves to greet this prodigal son upon his return, I was tremendously excited to see my mother, my humble home and the friends of my youth.

But my trip to the Transkei had a second motive: my arrival coincided with the meeting of a special committee appointed to oversee the transfer of the Transkeian Bungha system to that of the Bantu Authorities. While the Bungha was the most influential political body in the Transkei, its resolutions were advisory – the Bungha was only as powerful as the whites permitted it to be. Yet the Bantu Authorities Act would replace it with an even more represssive system.

On the night of my arrival, I briefly met a number of Transkeian councillors and my nephew Daliwonga, who was playing a leading part in persuading the Bungha to accept Bantu Authorities, for the new order would increase his power.

Over the next fortnight I moved back and forth between Qunu and Mqhekezweni, staying by turns with my mother and No-England, the regent's widow. The visit restored me and revived my feelings for the place in which I grew up. But in my discussions with Daliwonga we came no closer to each other's position. On family issues we remained friends; politically, we were in opposite camps.

Later, I drove on to Cape Town for a two-week stay. On the last day, I went to the offices of *New Age* to see some old friends and discuss their editorial policy. As I walked up the steps I could hear angry voices. I recognized the voice of Fred Carneson, the manager of the newspaper and its guiding spirit. I also heard the gruff voices of the security police. I later discovered that this had not been an isolated incident but part of the largest nationwide raid undertaken in South African history. Armed with warrants authorizing the seizure of anything regarded as evidence of high treason, sedition or violations of the Suppression of Communism Act, the police searched more than five hundred people in their homes and offices around the country. My office in Johannesburg was searched, as well as the homes of Dr Moroka, Father Huddleston and Professor Matthews. The raid signalled the first move in the state's new and even more repressive strategy.

I made good time on the way back to Johannesburg from Cape Town and arrived home just before supper, where I was met with excited cries from my children, who well knew that I was a father bearing gifts. One by one, I handed out the presents I had purchased in Cape Town and patiently answered the questions my children had for me about the trip. Though not a true holiday, it had the same effect: I felt rejuvenated and ready to take up the fight once more.

Immediately upon my return I reported on my trip to the Working Committee of the ANC. I did not give them good news. I said the Transkei was not a well organized ANC

The homelands were effectively reservoirs of cheap labour for white industry. In the Transkei (above) and other locations where displaced Africans were settled, camps were established without the backup of even basic amenities or infrastructure.

area and the power of the security police would soon immobilize what little influence the ANC had. I put forth an alternative that I knew would be unpopular. Why shouldn't the ANC participate in the new Bantu Authority structures as a means of remaining in touch with the masses of the people? In time, such participation would become a platform for our own ideas and policies.

Any suggestion of participating in apartheid structures in any way was automatically met with angry opposition. In my early days, I, too, would have strenuously objected. But my sense of the country was that relatively few people were ready to make sacrifices to join the struggle. We should meet the people on their own terms, even if that meant appearing to collaborate. My idea was that our movement should be a great tent that included as many people as possible.

At the time, however, my report was given short shrift because of another related report with greater ramifications. The publication of the report of the Tomlinson Commission for the Socio-Economic Development of the Bantu Areas had set off a nationwide debate. The government-created commission proposed a plan for the development of the so-called Bantu Areas or Bantustans. The result was in fact a blueprint for 'separate development' or Grand Apartheid.

The Bantustan system had been conceived by Dr H.F. Verwoerd, the minister of native affairs, as a way of muting international criticism of South African racial policies but at the same time institutionalizing apartheid. The Bantustans, or reserves as they were also known, would be separate ethnic enclaves or homelands for all African citizens. The idea was to preserve the status quo where three million whites owned 87 per cent of the land, and relegate the eight million Africans to the remaining 13 per cent.

The government's intention in creating the homeland system was to keep the Transkei – and other African areas – as reservoirs of cheap labour for white industry. At the same time, the covert goal of the government was to create an African middle class to blunt the appeal of the ANC and the liberation struggle.

Despite the encroaching darkness and my pessimism about the government's policies, I was thinking about the future. In February 1956 I returned to the Transkei to purchase a plot of land in Umtata. I have always thought a man should own a house near the place he was born, where he might find a restfulness that eludes him elsewhere.

In March 1956, after several months of relative freedom, I received my third ban, which restricted me to Johannesburg for five years and prohibited me from attending meetings for that same period.

But this time my attitude towards my bans had changed radically. When I was first banned, I abided by the rules and regulations of my persecutors. I had now developed contempt for these restrictions. I was not going to let my involvement in the struggle and the scope of my political activities be determined by the enemy I was fighting against. To allow my activities to be circumscribed by my opponent was a form of defeat, and I resolved not to become my own jailer.

Waiting to be moved from Sophiatown, 1955, at the end of the anti-removal campaign.

The ACCUSED — DECEMBER 1956

Treason

Just after dawn on the morning of 5 December 1956, I was woken by a loud knocking on my door. I dressed quickly and found security officer Rousseau and two policemen. He produced a search warrant, and they immediately began to comb through the entire house looking for incriminating papers or documents. After forty-five minutes, Rousseau matter-of-factly said, 'Mandela, we have a warrant for your arrest. Come with me.' I looked at the warrant, and the words leapt out at me: HIGH TREASON.

After a brief stop at the police station, we went to my office, which they searched for another forty-five minutes. From there, I was taken to Marshall Square prison. A number of my colleagues were already there, having been arrested earlier that morning. Over the next few hours, more friends and comrades began to trickle in. This was the swoop the government had long been planning. All told, there were one hundred and five Africans, twenty-one Indians, twenty-three whites and seven Coloureds. Almost the entire executive leadership of the ANC, both banned and unbanned, had been arrested. The government, at long last, had made its move.

We were soon moved to the Johannesburg Prison, popularly known as the Fort, a bleak, castle-like structure located on a hill. Upon admission, we were taken to an outdoor quadrangle and ordered to strip completely and line up against the wall. We were forced to stand there for more than an hour, shivering in the breeze and feeling awkward – priests, professors, doctors, lawyers, businessmen, men of middle or old age. A white doctor finally appeared and asked whether any of us was ill. We were ordered to dress, and then escorted to two large cells with cement floors and no furniture. The cells had recently been painted and reeked of paint fumes. We were each given three

thin blankets plus a sisal mat. Each cell had only one floor-level latrine, which was completely exposed. It is said that no one truly knows a nation until one has been inside its jails. A nation should not be judged by how it treats its highest citizens, but its lowest ones – and South Africa treated its imprisoned African citizens like animals.

On 19 December we appeared for our preparatory examination at the Drill Hall in Johannesburg, a military structure not normally used as a court of justice. The government was charging us with high treason and a countrywide conspiracy to use violence to overthrow the present government and replace it with a communist state. The punishment was death.

The purpose of a preparatory examination was to determine whether the government's charges were sufficient to put us on trial in the Supreme Court. That first day, the magistrate was Mr F.C.A. Wessel, the chief magistrate from Bloemfontein. Our supporters and organization had assembled a formidable defence team, including Bram Fischer, Norman Rosenberg, Israel Maisels, Maurice Franks and Vernon Berrangé.

The state cited the Freedom Charter as both proof of our communist intentions and evidence of our plot to overthrow the existing authorities. The charge was of high treason. On the fourth day, we were released on bail. Court was to resume in early January.

The treason trial. We were taken to the Drill Hall in sealed police vans escorted by half a dozen troop carriers filled with armed soldiers. One would have thought a full-scale civil war was under way from the precautions the state was taking with us.

In the mid 1950s, my marriage to Evelyn had begun to unravel. My devotion to the ANC and the struggle was unremitting. This disturbed Evelyn. She had always assumed that politics was a youthful diversion, that I would someday return to the Transkei and practise there as a lawyer. Even as that possibility became remote, she never resigned herself to the fact that Johannesburg would be our home, or let go of the idea that we might move back to Umtata. She encouraged Daliwonga's efforts to persuade me to come back to Umtata. We had many arguments about this, and I patiently explained to her that politics was not a distraction but my lifework, that it was an essential part of my being. She could not accept this. A man and a woman who hold such different views of their respective roles in life cannot remain close. We had irreconcilable differences. I never lost my respect and admiration for her, but in the end we could not make our marriage work.

On 9 January 1957 we once again assembled in the Drill Hall. It was the defence's turn to refute the state's charges. After summarizing the Crown's case against us, Vernon Berrangé, our lead counsel, announced our argument. 'The defence,' he said, 'will strenuously repudiate that the terms of the Freedom Charter are treasonable or criminal. On the contrary, the defence will contend that the ideas and beliefs which are expressed in this

charter are shared by the overwhelming majority of mankind of all races and colours, and also by the overwhelming majority of the citizens of this country.' We had decided that we were not merely going to prove that we were innocent of treason, but that this was a political trial in which the government was persecuting us for taking actions that were morally justified.

To support the allegation that we intended to replace the existing government with a Soviet-style state, the Crown relied on the evidence of Professor Andrew Murray, head of the Department of Political Science at the University of Cape Town. Murray labelled many of the documents seized from us, including the Freedom Charter itself, as communistic.

Professor Murray seemed relatively knowledgeable, until Berrangé began his cross-examination. Berrangé said that he wanted to read Murray a number of passages from various documents and then ask Murray to label them as communistic or not. The first passage concerned the need for ordinary workers to cooperate with each other and not exploit one another. Communistic, Murray said. Berrangé said the statement had been made by the former premier of South Africa, Dr Malan. Berrangé proceeded to read two other statements, both of which Professor Murray described as communistic. These passages had been uttered by the American presidents Abraham Lincoln and Woodrow Wilson. The highlight came with a passage that the professor described as 'communism straight from the shoulder'. Professor Murray himself had written this in the 1930s.

The treason trial. A massive crowd of our supporters was blocking traffic in Twist Street (above right); we could hear them cheering and singing, and they could hear us answering from inside the van. The trip became like a triumphal procession as the slow-moving van was rocked by the crowd.

Oswald Pirow, the Crown prosecutor (below left).

Finally, on 11 September, the prosecutor announced that the state's case in the preparatory examination was completed. The examination had lasted for the whole of 1957. Court adjourned and the defence began reviewing the evidence. Three months later, without explanation, the Crown announced that charges against sixty-one of the accused were to be dropped. Most of these defendants were relatively minor figures in the ANC, but also among them were Chief Luthuli and Oliver Tambo.

In January, when the government was scheduled to sum up its charges, the Crown brought in a new prosecutor, the formidable Oswald Pirow Q.C. Pirow was a former minister of justice and of defence and a pillar of National Party politics. The appointment was new evidence that the state was worried about the outcome and attached tremendous importance to a victory.

Before Pirow's summing-up, Berrangé announced that he would apply for our discharge on the ground that the state had not offered sufficient evidence against us. Pirow opposed this and quoted from several inflammatory speeches by the accused, informing the court that the police had unearthed more evidence of a highly dangerous conspiracy.

After thirteen months, the magistrate ruled that he had found 'sufficient reason' for putting us on trial in the Transvaal Supreme Court for high treason. Court adjourned in January with ninety-five remaining defendants committed to stand trial. When the actual trial would begin, we did not know.

One afternoon, during a recess in the preparatory examination, I drove a friend to the medical school at the University of the Witwatersrand. As I passed a bus stop, I noticed out of the corner of my eye a lovely young woman waiting for the bus. I was struck by her beauty, and I turned my head to get a better look at her.

Some weeks later, I popped in to see Oliver and there was this same young woman with her brother, sitting in front of his desk. Oliver introduced me to them and explained that they were visiting him on a legal matter.

Her name was Nomzamo Winifred Madikizela, known as Winnie. She was working as the first black female social worker at Baragwanath Hospital. The moment I first glimpsed Winnie Nomzamo, I knew that I wanted to have her as my wife.

I telephoned Winnie the next day at the hospital and asked her for help in raising money for the Treason Trial Defence Fund from the Jan Hofmeyr School. It was merely a pretext to invite her to lunch. Winnie was dazzling, and even the fact that she had never before tasted curry and drank glass after glass of water to cool her palate only added to her charm.

Hundreds of women
marched against
the pass laws, 1957, and
many were arrested.

Shortly after I filed for divorce from Evelyn, I told Winnie she should have a fitting for a wedding dress and suggested she inform her parents that we were to be married. Winnie has laughingly told people that I never proposed to her, but I always told her that I asked her on our very first date and simply took it for granted from that day forward.

The Treason Trial was in its second year and it put a suffocating weight on our law practice. The Mandela and Tambo firm was falling apart as we could not be there, and both Oliver and I were experiencing grave financial difficulties. I told Winnie it was more than likely that we would have to live on her small salary as a social worker. Winnie understood, and said she was prepared to take the risk and throw in her lot with me.

The wedding took place on 14 June 1958. I applied for a relaxation of my banning orders and was given six days' leave of absence from Johannesburg. I also arranged for *lobola*, the traditional brideprice, to be paid to Winnie's father.

After the ceremony in Bizana, a piece of the wedding cake was wrapped up for the bride to bring to the groom's ancestral home for the second part of the wedding. But it was never to be, for my leave of absence was up and we had to return to Johannesburg. Winnie carefully stored the cake in anticipation of that day. At our house, No. 8115 Orlando West, a large party of friends and family were there to welcome us back.

The state had not weakened in its resolve to impose passes on women. Although the government now called passes 'reference books', women weren't fooled: they could still be fined £10 or imprisoned for a month for failing to produce their 'reference book'. In 1957, spurred by the efforts of the ANC Women's League, women all across the country, in rural areas and in cities, reacted with fury to the state's insistence that they carry passes. Police arrested hundreds of the women.

The introduction of the women's pass led to an enormous protest

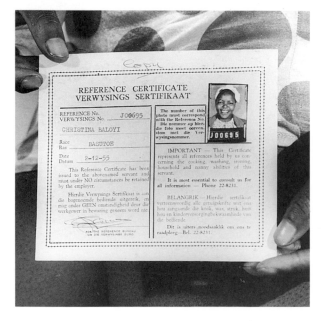

Not long after these arrests, Winnie quietly informed me that she intended to join the group of Orlando women who would be protesting the following day at the pass office. While I was pleased at her sense of commitment and admired her courage, I was also wary. Winnie had become increasingly politicized since our marriage, and had joined the Orlando West branch of the ANC's Women's League, all of which I encouraged.

I told her I welcomed her decision, but that I had to warn her about the seriousness of her action. If she was arrested she was certain to be sacked by her employer, the provincial administration – we both knew it was her small income that was supporting the household – and that she could probably never work again as a social worker. Finally, she was pregnant, and I warned her of the physical hardship and humiliations of jail. I felt responsibility, both as a

husband and as a leader of the struggle, to be as clear as possible about the ramifications of her action.

Hundreds of women converged on the Central Pass Office in downtown Johannesburg. They sang, marched and chanted. Within minutes they were surrounded by armed police, who arrested all of them, packed them into vans and drove them to Marshall Square police station. All told, more than a thousand women were arrested. I knew this because Mandela and Tambo were called on to represent most of the women who had been arrested. I quickly made my way to Marshall Square to visit the prisoners and arrange bail. I managed to see Winnie and I told her I was proud of her.

Supporters outside the
Old Synagogue during the
treason trial (right).

The interior of the court
in Pretoria, converted from
a synagogue (below right).

For six months – ever since the end of the preparatory hearings in January – we had been preparing for our formal trial, which was to start in August 1958. The government set up a special high court – Mr Justice F.L. Rumpff, president of the three-man court, Mr Justice Kennedy and Mr Justice Ludorf. While Judge Rumpff was able and better informed than the average white South African, he was rumoured to be a member of the Broederbond, a secret Afrikaner organization whose aim was to solidify Afrikaner power. Judge Ludorf was a well-known member of the National Party, as was Judge Kennedy. Kennedy had a reputation as a hanging judge, having sent a group of twenty-three Africans to the gallows for the murder of two white policemen.

Shortly before the case resumed, the state announced that the venue of the trial was to be shifted from Johannesburg to Pretoria, thirty-six miles away. The trial would now take up even more of our time and money. Changing the venue was also an attempt to crush our spirits by separating us from our natural supporters. Pretoria was the home of the National Party, and the ANC barely had a presence there.

Nearly all the ninety-two accused commuted to Pretoria in a lumbering, uncomfortable bus, with stiff wooden slats for seats, which left every day at six in the morning and took two hours to reach the court.

Once more we were privileged to have a brilliant and aggressive defence team, ably led by advocate Israel Maisels, and assisted by Bram Fischer, Rex Welsh, Vernon

The accused were bussed each day from Johannesburg to Pretoria for the treason trial.

Berrangé, Sydney Kentridge, Tony O'Dowd and G. Nicholas. On the opening day of the trial, Issy Maisels applied for the recusal of Judges Ludorf and Rumpff on the grounds that both had conflicts of interest that prevented them from being fair arbiters of our case. Rumpff, as the judge at the 1952 Defiance Trial, had already adjudicated on certain aspects of the present indictment and therefore it was not in the interest of justice that he try this case. Ludorf was prejudiced, because he had represented the government in 1954 as a lawyer for the police when Harold Wolpe had sought a court interdict to eject the police from a meeting of the Congress of the People.

This was a dangerous strategy, for there were far worse judges who could replace them. In fact, while we were keen to have Ludorf step down, we secretly hoped that Rumpff, whom we respected as an honest broker, would decide not to.

Judge Ludorf announced that he would withdraw, but Rumpff refused and instead offered the assurance that his judgment in the Defiance case would have no influence on him in this one. We were happy with his decision. To replace Ludorf, the state appointed Mr Justice Bekker, a man we liked right from the start and who was not linked to the National Party.

We then began a long and detailed argument contesting the indictment itself. We claimed that the indictment was vague and lacked particulars. We also argued that the planning of violence was necessary to prove high treason, and the prosecution needed to provide examples. It became apparent by the end of our argument that the three judges agreed. In August, the court quashed one of the two charges under the Suppression of Communism Act. Then, on 13 October, the Crown suddenly announced the withdrawal of the indictment altogether. But we were too well versed in the devious ways of the state to celebrate. A month later the prosecution issued a new, more carefully worded, indictment and announced that the trial would proceed against only thirty of the accused; the others would be tried later. I was among the first thirty, all of whom were members of the ANC.

Under the new indictment, the prosecution was now required to prove the intention to act violently. The legal sparring continued until the middle of 1959, when the court dismissed the Crown's indictment against the remaining sixty-one accused. Despite the defence's successes in showing the shoddiness of the government's case, the state was obdurately persistent. As the minister of justice said, 'This trial will be proceeded with, no matter how many millions of pounds it costs. What does it matter how long it takes?'

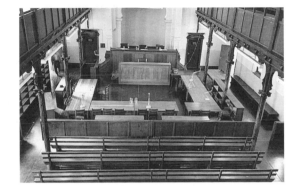

On 4 February 1958, my daughter Zenani was born. My relative, Chief Mdingi, suggested the name Zenani, which means 'What have you brought to the world?' – a poetic name that embodies a challenge, suggesting that one must contribute something to society. It is a name one has to live up to.

On 6 April 1959, the Pan-Africanist Congress launched itself as an Africanist organization that expressly rejected the multiracialism of the ANC. Like those of us who had formed the Youth League fifteen years before, the founders of the new organization thought the ANC was insufficiently militant, out of touch with the masses and dominated by non-Africans.

Robert Sobukwe was elected president and Potlako Leballo became national secretary, both of them former ANC Youth Leaguers. The PAC presented a manifesto and a constitution, along with Sobukwe's opening address, in which he called for a 'government of the Africans by the Africans and for the Africans'. The PAC declared that it intended to overthrow white supremacy and establish a government Africanist in origin, socialist in content and democratic in form. They disavowed communism in all its forms and considered whites and Indians 'foreign minority groups' or 'aliens' who had no natural place in South Africa. South Africa was for Africans, and no one else.

It was opposed to interracial cooperation, in large part because it believed that white communists and Indians had come to dominate the ANC.

Because of the PAC's anti-communism, it became the darling of the Western press and the American State Department. Even the National Party saw a potential ally in the PAC. Both the National Party and the American State Department saw fit to exaggerate the size and importance of the new organization for their own ends.

Winnie Mandela in the Transkei with Paramount Chief Sabata, one of the protestors against the Bantustan policy.

In 1959, Parliament passed the Promotion of Bantu Self Government Act, which created eight separate ethnic Bantustans. This was the foundation of what the state called *groot* or grand apartheid. At roughly the same time, the government introduced the deceptively named Extension of University Education Act, another leg of grand apartheid, which barred nonwhites from racially 'open' universities. De Wet Nel, the minister of Bantu administration and development, said that the welfare of every individual and population group could best be developed within its own national community. Africans, he said, could never be integrated into the white community.

The immorality of the Bantustan policy, whereby 70 per cent of the people would be apportioned only 13 per cent of the land, was obvious. Under the new policy, even though two-thirds of Africans lived in so-called white areas, they could have citizenship only in their own 'tribal homelands'. Verwoerd said the creation of the Bantustans would engender so much goodwill that they would never become the breeding grounds for rebellion.

In reality, it was quite the opposite. Protests erupted in Zeerust, Sekhukhuneland and eastern Pondoland, where government henchmen were assaulted and killed. Thembuland and Zululand fiercely resisted, and were among the last areas to yield. People were beaten, arrested, deported and imprisoned.

It was especially painful to me that in the Transkei, the wrath of the people was directed against my nephew and one-time mentor K.D. Matanzima. There was no doubt that Daliwonga was collaborating with the government and there were several assassination attempts against him.

On a number of occasions, tribesmen and kinsmen from the Transkei visited me to complain about chiefs collaborating with the government. Sabata was opposed to the Bantu Authorities and would not capitulate, but my visitors were afraid that Matanzima would depose him, which is eventually what happened.

On 3 August 1959, two years and eight months after our arrests, and after a full year of legal manoeuvring, the actual trial commenced in Pretoria.

This time, at long last, the trial was in earnest. On the morning of 11 October, as we were preparing to go to court, we heard an announcement that the prosecutor, Oswald Pirow, had died suddenly from a stroke. His death was a severe setback to the government, and the effectiveness of the Crown team diminished from that point on. Advocate de Vos became the new leader of the Crown's team, but could not match the eloquence or acuity of his predecessor.

Police conduct a pass
check. The December 1959
ANC conference was
held in Durban during
that city's dynamic anti-
pass demonstrations.
The conference voted
to initiate a massive
countrywide anti-pass
campaign, climaxing on
26 June with a great
bonfire of passes.

Shortly after Pirow's death, the prosecution concluded its submission of evidence. It was then that the prosecution began its examination of expert witnesses, commencing with the long-suffering Professor Murray, its supposed expert in communism. In a relentless cross-examination by Maisels, Murray admitted that the charter was in fact a humanitarian document that might well represent the natural reaction and aspirations of non-whites to the harsh conditions in South Africa.

The prosecution concluded its case on 10 March 1960 and we were to call our first witness for the defence four days later. There had been much speculation in the press that our first witness would be Chief Luthuli. The Crown apparently believed that as well, for there was great consternation when, on 14 March, our first witness was Dr Wilson Conco.

Conco was the son of a Zulu cattle farmer from the Ixopo district of Natal. In addition to being a practising physician, he had been one of the founders of the Youth League, an active participant in the Defiance Campaign and the treasurer of the ANC. Dr Conco proved a calm and articulate witness who reaffirmed the ANC's commitment to non-violence.

Chief Luthuli was next. With his dignity and sincerity, he made a deep impression on the court. He carefully outlined the evolution of the ANC's policy, putting things simply and clearly, and his former positions as teacher and chief imparted an added gravity and authority to his words. As a devout Christian, he was the perfect person to discuss how the ANC had sincerely strived for racial harmony.

But on 21 March the chief's testimony was interrupted by a shattering event outside the courtroom. On that day, the country was rocked by an occurrence of such magnitude that when Chief Luthuli returned to testify a month later, the courtroom – and all of South Africa – was a different place. That event was Sharpeville.

The December 1959 ANC annual conference was held in Durban during that city's anti-pass demonstrations. The conference unanimously voted to initiate a massive countrywide anti-pass campaign beginning on 31 March and climaxing on 26 June with a great bonfire of passes.

ANC officials toured the country, talking to the branches. ANC field-workers spread the word in townships and factories. Leaflets, stickers and posters were printed and circulated and posted in trains and buses.

The mood of the country was grim. The state was threatening to ban the organization, with cabinet ministers warning the ANC that it would soon be battered with 'an ungloved fist'. Elsewhere in Africa the freedom struggle was marching on. In 1960 seventeen former colonies in Africa were scheduled to become independent states. In February, the British prime minister Harold Macmillan visited South Africa and gave a speech before Parliament in which he talked of 'winds of change' sweeping Africa.

The PAC knew of the ANC's anti-pass campaign and had been invited to join, but instead they sought to sabotage us. The PAC announced that it was launching its own anti-pass campaign on 21 March, ten days before ours was to begin. It was a blatant case of opportunism.

Four days before the scheduled demonstration, Sobukwe invited us to join with the PAC. Sobukwe's offer was a tactical move to prevent the PAC from being criticized for not including us. He made the offer at the eleventh hour, and we declined. On the morning of 21 March Sobukwe and his executive walked to the Orlando police station to turn themselves in for arrest. They believed the defiers would receive sentences of a few weeks, but Sobukwe was sentenced to three years' imprisonment without the option of a fine.

The response to the PAC's call in Johannesburg was minimal. No demonstrations at all took place in Durban, Port Elizabeth or East London. But in Evaton they mustered the support of the entire township as several hundred men presented themselves for arrest without passes. Cape Town saw one of the biggest anti-pass demonstrations in the history of the city. In Langa township, outside Cape Town, some thirty thousand people, led by the young student, Philip Kgosana, gathered and were spurred to rioting by a police baton-charge. Two people were killed. But the last of the areas where demonstrations took place was the most calamitous and the one whose name still echoes with tragedy: Sharpeville, a small township about thirty-five miles south of Johannesburg.

The shootings at Sharpeville provoked national turmoil and a government crisis. Outraged protests came in from across the globe, including one from the American State Department. For the first time, the UN Security Council intervened in South African affairs, blaming the government for the shootings and urging it to initiate measures to bring about racial equality. The Johannesburg stock exchange plunged, and capital started to flow out of the country. South African whites began making plans to emigrate.

The massacre at Sharpeville created a new situation in the country. In spite of the opportunism of their leaders, the PAC rank and file displayed great courage and fortitude in their demonstrations at Sharpeville and Langa. We in the ANC had to acknowledge the events in some way and give the people an outlet for their anger and grief. We conveyed our plans to Chief Luthuli. On 26 March, in Pretoria, the chief publicly burned his pass, calling on others to do the same. He announced a nationwide stay-at-home for 28 March, a national Day of Mourning and protest for the atrocities at Sharpeville. In Orlando, Duma Nokwe and I then burned our passes before hundreds of people and dozens of press photographers.

Two days later, on the 28th, the country responded magnificently as several hundred thousand Africans observed the chief's call. In Cape Town a crowd of fifty thousand met in Langa township to protest against the shootings. Rioting broke out in many areas. The government declared a State of Emergency, suspending habeas corpus and assuming sweeping powers to act against all forms of subversion. South Africa was now under martial law.

At 1.30 in the morning on 30 March I was awakened by sharp knocks at my door. 'The time has come,' I said to myself as I opened the door to find armed security police. They turned the house upside down, taking virtually every piece of paper they could find. I was then arrested without a warrant, and given no opportunity to call my lawyer.

I was taken to Newlands police station in Sophiatown. Inside I found a number of my colleagues, and over the course of the night more arrived; by morning we totalled forty in all. We were placed in a tiny cell with a single drainage hole in the floor which could be flushed only from the outside. We were given no blankets, no food, no mats and no toilet paper. The hole regularly became blocked and the stench in the room was insufferable.

At 3 p.m., more than twelve hours after most of us had arrived, we were delivered a container of thin mealie pap and no utensils. At 6 p.m. we received sleeping-mats and blankets. I do not think words can do justice to a description of the foulness and filthiness of this bedding. The blankets were encrusted with dried blood and vomit, ridden with lice, vermin and cockroaches, and reeked with a stench that actually competed with the stink of the drain.

Sharpeville, March 21 1960. Sharpeville was a small township about thirty-five miles south of Johannesburg in the grim industrial complex around Vereeniging. In the early afternoon, a crowd of several thousand surrounded the police station. The demonstrators were controlled and unarmed. The police force of seventy-five was greatly outnumbered and panicky. No one heard warning shots or an order to shoot, but suddenly the police opened fire on the crowd and continued to shoot as the demonstrators turned and ran in fear. When the area had cleared, sixty-nine Africans lay dead, most of them shot in the back as they were fleeing. All told, more than seven hundred shots had been fired into the crowd, wounding more than four hundred people, including dozens of women and children. It was a massacre, and the next day press photos displayed the savagery on front pages around the world.

The next morning we were informed that we had to leave to attend the Treason Trial in Pretoria. I did not know whether to laugh or despair, but in the midst of this thirty-six hours of mistreatment and the declaration of a State of Emergency, the government still saw fit to take us back to Pretoria to continue their desperate case against us.

In the meantime, court resumed in our absence, on 31 March, but the witness box was empty. Chief Luthuli had been in the middle of his evidence, and Judge Rumpff asked for an explanation for his absence. The chief had been taken into custody. Judge Rumpff expressed irritation and said he did not see why the State of Emergency should stand in the way of his trial. He demanded that the police bring the chief to court so that he could resume his testimony, and court was adjourned.

When we were called back into session that morning, Judge Rumpff was informed that the police refused to bring the chief to court. The judge then adjourned court for the day, and we expected to go home. But we were all once again arrested.

That night, we were joined by detainees from other parts of the Transvaal. The countrywide police raid had led to the detention without trial of more than two thousand people. A call-up of soldiers had been announced, and units of the army had been mobilized and stationed in strategic areas around the country. On 8 April both the ANC and the PAC were declared illegal organizations under the Suppression of Communism Act. Overnight, being a member of the ANC had become a felony punishable by a term in jail and a fine. The penalty for furthering the aims of the ANC was imprisonment for up to ten years. The struggle had entered a new phase. We were now outlaws.

On 25 April, the day before the trial was to resume, Issy Maisels called us together to discuss the effect the State of Emergency was having on the trial. Consultations between the accused and our lawyers had become virtually impossible. The defence team proposed that they withdraw from the case in protest. Maisels explained the serious implications of such a withdrawal. Under the hostile atmosphere at the time, the judges might see fit to give us longer terms of imprisonment. The resolution was unanimously endorsed, and it was agreed that Duma Nokwe and I would help in preparing the case in the absence of our lawyers. I was in favour of this dramatic gesture, for it highlighted the iniquities of the State of Emergency.

On 26 April Duma Nokwe, the first African advocate in the Transvaal, rose in court and made the sensational announcement that the accused were instructing defence counsel to withdraw from the case, after which the defence team filed out of the synagogue. This shocked the three-judge panel, who warned us about the dangers of conducting our own defence. But we were angry and eager to take on the state. For the next five months, until the virtual end of the Emergency, we conducted our own defence.

It is never easy to prepare a case from prison, and in this instance we were hampered by the customary apartheid barriers. The accused needed to be able to meet, but prison regulations prohibited meetings between male and female prisoners, and between black and white. After protracted negotiations with the prison authorities, we were permitted to have consultations under very strict conditions. The first stipulation was that there could be no physical contact between white and black prisoners, and between male and female prisoners. The authorities erected an iron grille to separate Helen Joseph and Leon Levy (as whites) from us and a second partition to separate them from Lilian Ngoyi and Bertha Mashaba (as African women), who were also participating. Helen needed to be separated from Lilian because of colour, and from us because of sex and colour.

My own testimony began on 3 August. After three years of silence, banning and internal exile, I looked forward to the chance to speak out. During my evidence I preached moderation and reaffirmed the ANC's commitment to non-violent struggle. The state was determined to prove that I was a dangerous, violence-spouting communist. While I was not a communist or a member of the party, I did not want to be seen as distancing myself from my communist allies. Although I could have been sent back to jail for voicing such views, I did not hesitate to reaffirm the tremendous support the communists had given us.

The Emergency was lifted on the last day of August. We would be going home for the first time in five months. When people in Johannesburg heard about the end of the Emergency, they drove up on the chance that we might be released; when we were let go, we were met with a jubilant reception from friends and family. Winnie had got a ride to Pretoria and our reunion was joyous. I had not held my wife in five months or seen her smile with joy. For the first time in five months, I slept in my own bed that night.

Helen Joseph, Secretary of the South African Women's Federation, and one of the accused.

ANC Women's League President Lilian Ngoyi.

Even after the end of the Emergency, the trial continued for another nine months until 29 March 1961. In many ways, these were the glory days for the accused, for our own people were on the stand fearlessly enunciating ANC policy.

In October the redoubtable Professor Matthews was called as our final witness. He treated the prosecutors as though they were errant students. He explained that the African people knew that a non-violent struggle would entail suffering but had chosen it because they prized freedom above all else. People, he said, will willingly undergo the severest suffering in order to free themselves from oppression. With Professor Matthews in the dock, the defence ended on a high note. After he finished testifying, Justice Kennedy shook his hand and expressed the hope that they would meet again under better circumstances.

After the lifting of the Emergency, the National Executive decided to carry on from underground. We were now an illegal organization. For those who continued to participate, politics went from being a risky occupation to a truly perilous one.

Though Mandela and Tambo had closed its doors, I continued to do what legal work I could. During this period I hardly had time for meals and saw very little of my family. I would stay late in Pretoria preparing for our case, or rush back to handle another case. Winnie was pregnant again, and infinitely patient. She was hoping her husband might actually be there when she gave birth, but it was not to be. We named our second daughter Zindziswa, after the daughter of the poet laureate of the Xhosa people, Samuel Mqhayi.

The Crown took over a month to do its summing up. In March it was our turn. Issy Maisels categorically refuted the charges of violence. 'We admit that there is a question of non-cooperation and passive resistance,' he said. 'We shall say quite frankly that if non-cooperation and passive resistance constitute high treason, then we are guilty. But these are plainly not encompassed in the law of treason.'

Maisels's argument was continued by Bram Fischer, but on 23 March the bench cut short Bram's concluding argument and asked for a week's adjournment. We were to return to court six days later for what we presumed would be the verdict. In the meantime, I had work to do.

My bans were due to expire two days after the adjournment. It would be the first time in nearly five years that I would be free to leave Johannesburg. That weekend was the long-planned All-in Conference in Pietermaritzburg. Its aim was to agitate for a national constitutional convention for all South Africans. I was secretly scheduled to be the main speaker at the conference.

The day before I was to leave, the National Working Committee met secretly to discuss strategy. It was decided that if we were not convicted, I would go underground to travel about the country organizing the proposed national convention. Only someone operating full-time from underground would be free from the paralysing restrictions imposed by the enemy. It was decided that I would surface at certain events, hoping for a maximum of publicity, to show that the ANC was still fighting. It was not a proposal that came as a surprise to me, nor was it one I particularly relished, but it was something I knew I had to do.

When I returned home from the meeting it was as though Winnie could read my thoughts. She knew that I was about to embark on a life that neither of us wanted. I asked her to pack a small suitcase for me. I would return to Pretoria for what would probably be the verdict on Monday. No matter what the result, I would not be returning home: if we were convicted, I would go to prison; if we were discharged, I would immediately go underground.

Fourteen hundred delegates from all over the country converged on Pietermaritzburg for the All-in Conference. When I walked out on stage on Saturday evening, 25 March, it had been nearly five years since I had been free to give a speech on a public platform. I was met with a joyous reaction.

The All-in Conference called for a national convention of elected representatives of all adult men and women on an equal basis to determine a new non-racial democratic constitution for South Africa. A National Action Council was elected to communicate this demand to the government. If the government failed to call such a convention, we would call a countrywide three-day stay-away beginning on 29 May to coincide with the declaration of South Africa as a republic.

In October 1960 the government had held an all-white referendum on whether South Africa should become a republic. This was one of the long-cherished dreams of Afrikaner nationalism, to cast off ties with the country they had fought against in the Anglo-Boer war. The pro-republic sentiment won with 52 per cent of the vote, and the proclamation of the republic was set for 31 May 1961. We set our stay-at-home on the date of the proclamation to indicate that, for us, such a change was merely cosmetic.

Directly after the conference I sent Prime Minister Verwoerd a letter in which I formally enjoined him to call a national constitutional convention. I warned him that if he failed to call it we would stage the country's most massive three-day strike ever, beginning on 29 May. I also issued press statements affirming that the strike was a peaceful and non-violent stay-at-home.

On 29 March 1961, the day of the long-anticipated verdict in the Treason Trial, a crowd of supporters and press people jostled to get inside. The court said the prosecution had failed to prove that the ANC was a communist organization or that the Freedom Charter envisioned a communist state. Justice Rumpff said, 'The accused are accordingly found not guilty and are discharged.' The verdict was an embarrassment to the government, both at home and abroad. Yet the lesson they took away was not that we had legitimate grievances but that they needed to be far more ruthless.

Addressing the Pietermaritzburg All-in Conference, 25 March 1961. When I walked out on stage it had been nearly five years since I had been free to give a speech on a public platform. I was met with a joyous reaction.

The Black Pimpernel

I sat for this portrait, (opposite) wearing an authentic beaded necklace of the Thembu clan, while on the run, when I was known as the Black Pimpernel.

At Algerian Military Headquarters during our visit to the independent African states, 1962 (below).

I did not return home after the verdict. Although others were in a festive mood and eager to celebrate, I knew the authorities could strike at any moment, and I did not want to give them the opportunity.

Walter and Duma saw me off on the first leg of my journey, which was to take me to Port Elizabeth. There I met Govan Mbeki and Raymond Mhlaba to discuss the new underground structures of the organization. We met at the house of Dr Masla Pather, who would later be sentenced to two years in prison for allowing us to meet at his home.

Later I joined a secret meeting of the ANC National Executive and the joint executives of the Congress movement in Durban to discuss whether the planned action should take the form of a stay-at-home or a fully-fledged strike with organized pickets and demonstrations. Those who argued for the strike said that the stay-at-home strategy we had used since 1950 had outlasted its usefulness, that at a time when the PAC was appealing to the masses, more militant forms of the struggle were necessary. The alternative view, which I advocated, was that stay-at-homes allowed us to strike at the enemy while preventing him from striking back. The decision was for a stay-at-home.

Living underground requires a seismic psychological shift. One has to plan every action, however small and seemingly insignificant. Nothing is innocent. Everything is questioned. I became a creature of the night. I would keep to my hideout during the day, and emerge to do my work when it became dark. I operated mainly from Johannesburg, but I would travel as necessary. I stayed in empty flats, in people's houses, wherever I could be alone and inconspicuous. I welcomed the opportunity to be by myself, to plan, to think, to plot. But one can have too much solitude. I missed my wife and family.

My most frequent disguise was as a chauffeur, chef or a 'garden boy'. I had a car and wore a chauffeur's cap with my overalls. The pose of chauffeur was convenient because I could travel under the pretext of driving my master's car.

During those early months, when there was a warrant for my arrest and I was being pursued by the police, my outlaw existence caught the imagination of the press. Articles claiming that I had been here and there were on the front pages. Roadblocks were instituted all over the country, but the police repeatedly came up empty-handed and so I was dubbed the Black Pimpernel.

I travelled secretly about the country: I was with Muslims in the Cape, with sugar-workers in Natal, with factory workers in Port Elizabeth. I moved through townships in different parts of the country attending secret meetings at night.

My time underground was mainly taken up in planning the 29 May stay-at-home. It was shaping up to be a virtual war between the state and the liberation movement. Two days before, the government staged the greatest peacetime show of force in South African history. The military exercised its largest call-up since the war. Police holidays were cancelled. Military units were stationed at the entrances and exits of townships.

On the first day of the stay-at home hundreds of thousands of people risked their jobs by not going to work, but the response as a whole appeared less than we had hoped. On the second day of the stay-at-home, after consultations with my colleagues, I called it off. That morning, in a safe flat in a white suburb I met various members of the local and foreign press, and I once again called the stay-at-home 'a tremendous success'. But I did not mask the fact that I believed a new day was dawning. I said, 'If the government reaction is to crush by naked force our non-violent struggle, we will have to reconsider our tactics. In my mind we are closing a chapter on this question of a non-violent policy.' It was a grave declaration, and I knew it.

The debate on the use of violence had been going on among us since early 1960. I had first discussed the armed struggle as far back as 1952 with Walter Sisulu. Now, I again conferred with him and we agreed that the organization had to set out on a new course. We decided that I should raise the issue of the armed struggle within the Working Committee, and I did so in a meeting in June of 1961.

The Executive meeting in Durban, like all ANC meetings at the time, was held in secret and at night in order to avoid the police. I suspected I would encounter difficulties because Chief Luthuli was to be in attendance and I knew of his moral commitment to non-violence. I was also wary because of the timing: I was raising the issue of violence so soon after the Treason Trial, where we had contended that for the ANC non-violence was an inviolate principle, not a tactic to be changed as conditions warranted. I myself believed precisely the opposite; that non-violence was a tactic that should be abandoned when it no longer worked.

At the meeting I argued that the state had given us no alternative to violence. I said it was wrong to subject our people to armed attacks by the state without offering them some

‘On one occasion, I was driving in town and stopped at a traffic light. I looked to my left and in an adjacent car saw Colonel Spengler, the chief of the Witwatersrand Security Branch. It would have been a great plum for him to catch the Black Pimpernel. ’

kind of alternative. I mentioned again that people on their own had taken up arms. Violence would begin whether we initiated it or not.

In the end the National Executive formally endorsed the preliminary decision of the Working Committee. The idea was that a military movement should be a separate and independent organ, linked to the ANC and under the overall control of the ANC, but fundamentally autonomous. There would be two separate streams of the struggle.

The following night a meeting of the joint Executive was scheduled in Durban. This would include the Indian Congress, the Coloured People's Congress, the South African Congress of Trade Unions and the Congress of Democrats. Although these other groups customarily accepted ANC decisions, I knew that some of my Indian colleagues would strenuously oppose the move towards violence.

We began our session at 8 p.m., and it was tumultuous. But, after a long and protracted discussion, the Congresses authorized me to go ahead and form a new military organization, separate from the ANC. The policy of the ANC would still be that of non-violence. I was authorized to join with whoever I wanted or needed to create this organization and would not be subject to the direct control of the mother organization.

This was a fateful step. For fifty years, the ANC had treated non-violence as a core principle, beyond question or debate. We were embarking on a new and more dangerous path, a path of organized violence, the results of which we did not and could not know. I, who had never been a soldier, who had never fought in battle, had been given the task of starting an army. The name of this new organization was Umkhonto we Sizwe (The Spear of the Nation) – or MK for short.

Winnie and our daughters Zenani and Zindzi (below). The loveliest times at the farm were when I was visited by my wife and family. Once the Goldreichs were in residence, Winnie would visit me at weekends. We were careful about her movements, and she would be picked up by one driver, dropped off at another place, and then picked up by a second driver before finally being delivered to the farm.

Although the Executive of the ANC did not allow white members, MK was not thus constrained. I immediately recruited Joe Slovo and along with Walter Sisulu we formed the High Command with myself as chairman. Through Joe, I enlisted the efforts of white Communist Party members who had already executed acts of sabotage such as cutting government telephone and communication lines. We recruited Jack Hodgson, who had fought in the Second World War and was a member of the Springbok Legion, and Rusty Bernstein, both party members. Jack became our first demolition expert. Our mandate was to wage acts of violence against the state – precisely what form those acts would take was yet to be decided. Our intention was to begin with what was least violent to individuals but most damaging to the state.

On 26 June 1961, our Freedom Day, I released a letter to South African newspapers from underground, once more calling for a national constitutional convention. I again proclaimed that a countrywide campaign of non-cooperation would be launched if the state failed to hold such a convention.

During those first few months underground I lived first with a family in Market

Street, and then in a flat in Berea with Wolfie Kodesh, a member of the Congress of Democrats and a reporter for *New Age*. I spent nearly two months in his flat, staying inside during the day with the blinds drawn reading and planning, leaving only for meetings or organizing sessions at night.

In October I moved to Liliesleaf Farm, located in Rivonia, a northern suburb of Johannesburg. The farmhouse and smallholdings had been purchased by the movement for the purpose of having a safe house.

I moved in under the pretext that I was the houseboy who would look after the place until my master took possession. I had taken the alias David Motsamayi, the name of one of my former clients. At the farm, I wore the simple blue overalls that were the uniform of the black male servant.

After a number of weeks I was joined at the farm by Raymond Mhlaba, who was a staunch trade unionist, a member of the Cape Executive and the Communist Party, and the first ANC leader to be arrested in the Defiance Campaign. He had been chosen by the ANC to be one of the first recruits for Umkhonto we Sizwe. He had come to prepare for his departure, with three others, for military training in the People's Republic of China. Ray stayed with me for a fortnight and I enlisted his assistance in writing the MK constitution. We were joined by Joe Slovo as well as Rusty Bernstein, who both had hands in drafting it.

Soon after this Arthur Goldreich and his family moved into the main house as official tenants and I took over the domestic worker's cottage. Arthur's presence provided a safe

An aerial view of the main house and outbuildings at Liliesleaf Farm, Rivonia, a northern suburb of Johannesburg.

cover for our activities. He was an artist and designer by profession, a member of the Congress of Democrats and one of the first members of MK. His politics were unknown to the police and he had never been questioned or raided.

The final addition to the regular group at the farm was Mr Jelliman, an amiable white pensioner and old friend of the movement who became the farm foreman. Jelliman brought in several young workers from Sekhukhuneland, and the place soon appeared to be like any other smallholding. He was not a member of the ANC, but he was loyal, discreet, and hard working. Much later, Jelliman risked his own life and livelihood in a courageous attempt to help me.

Winnie and the children were now able to visit me at weekends. We were careful about her movements, though the police were not yet following her everywhere. Ironically, we had more privacy at Liliesleaf than we ever had at home. The children could run about and play, and we were secure, however briefly, in this idyllic bubble.

In planning the direction and form that MK would take, we considered four types of violent activities: sabotage, guerrilla warfare, terrorism and open revolution. For a small and fledgling army, open revolution was inconceivable. Terrorism inevitably reflected poorly on those who used it, undermining any public support it might otherwise garner. Guerrilla warfare was a possibility, but since the ANC had been reluctant to embrace violence at all, it made sense to start with the form of violence that inflicted the least harm against individuals: sabotage.

Our strategy was to make selective forays against military installations, power plants, telephone lines and transportation links; targets that would not only hamper the military effectiveness of the state, but frighten National Party supporters, scare away foreign capital, and weaken the economy. This we hoped would bring the government to the bargaining table. Strict instructions were given to members of MK that we would countenance no loss of life. But if sabotage did not produce the results we wanted, we were prepared to move on to the next stage: guerrilla warfare and terrorism.

One warm December afternoon, while I sat in the kitchen at Liliesleaf Farm, I listened on the radio to the announcement that Chief Luthuli had been awarded the Nobel Peace Prize at a ceremony in Oslo. The government had issued him with a ten-day visa to leave the country and accept the award. I was enormously pleased. It represented a recognition in the West that our struggle was a moral one, one too long ignored by the great powers.

Police photographs of the interior of Liliesleaf Farm at the time of the raid, 11 July 1963.

The honour came at an awkward time, for it coincided with an announcement that seemed to call the award itself into question. The day after Luthuli returned from Oslo, a series of bombs exploded at electric power stations and government offices in Johannesburg, Port Elizabeth and Durban on the orders of the MK High Command. At the same time, thousands of leaflets with the new MK Manifesto were circulated all over the country announcing the birth of Umkhonto we Sizwe.

The explosions took the government by surprise. They condemned the sabotage as heinous crimes while at the same time deriding it as the work of foolish amateurs. The explosions also shocked white South Africans into the realization that they were sitting on top of a volcano. Black South Africans realized that the ANC was no longer an organization of passive resistance, but a powerful spear that would take the struggle to the heart of white power. We planned and executed another set of explosions two weeks later on New Year's Eve. The sound of bells tolling and sirens wailing symbolized a new era.

In December the ANC received an invitation from the Pan-African Freedom Movement for East, Central and Southern Africa (PAFMECSA) to attend its conference in Addis Ababa in February 1962. PAFMECSA, which later became the Organization of African Unity, aimed to draw together the independent states of Africa and promote the liberation movements on the continent.

The underground Executive asked me to lead the ANC delegation to the conference. My mission in Africa was broader than simply attending the conference; I was to arrange political and economic support for our new military force and, more important, military training for our men in as many places on the continent as possible. I was also determined to boost our reputation in the rest of Africa where we were still relatively unknown. The

On the orders of the MK High Command, in the early morning hours of 16 December – the day white South Africans used to celebrate as Dingane's Day – homemade bombs were exploded at electric power stations and government offices in Johannesburg, Port Elizabeth and Durban.

PAC had launched its own propaganda campaign and I was delegated to make our case wherever possible.

Before leaving, I secretly drove to Groutville to confer with the chief. Our meeting was disconcerting. As I have related, the chief was present at the creation of MK, and was as informed as any member of the National Executive about its development. But the chief was not well and his memory was not what it had once been. He chastised me for not consulting him about the formation of MK. I attempted to remind him of the discussions that we had in Durban about taking up violence, but he did not recall them. This is in large part why the story has gained currency that Chief Luthuli was not informed about the creation of MK and was deeply opposed to the ANC taking up violence. Nothing could be further from the truth.

I had spent the night before my departure with Winnie at the house of white friends in the northern suburbs, and she brought me a suitcase that she had packed. She was anxious about my leaving the country, but once again remained stoic. She behaved as much like a soldier as a wife.

The ANC had to arrange for me to travel to Dar es Salaam in Tanganyika, from where the flight to Addis Ababa would leave. The plan was for Walter, Kathrada, and Duma Nokwe to meet me at a secret rendezvous in Soweto and bring me my credentials for the trip. It would also be a moment for last-minute consultations before I left the country.

Ahmed Kathrada arrived at the appointed hour, but Walter and Duma were extremely late. I finally had to make alternative arrangements and Kathy [Kathrada] managed to locate someone to drive me to Bechuanaland, where I would charter a plane. I later learned that Walter and Duma had been arrested.

Our destination was Lobatse, near the South African border. We passed through the border without a problem and arrived in Lobatse in the late afternoon. I was soon joined by Joe Matthews, who had come from Basutoland, and I insisted we should make haste for Dar es Salaam. A plane was arranged, and our first destination was a town in northern Bechuanaland called Kasane, strategically situated near a point where the borders of four countries met – Bechuanaland, Northern and Southern Rhodesia, and South West Africa, as these colonies were then known.

From Kasane we went on to Mbeya, a Tanganyikan town near the Northern Rhodesian border. We booked in at a local hotel and found a crowd of blacks and whites sitting on the veranda making polite conversation. Never before had I been in a public place or hotel where there was no colour bar. I then truly realized that I was in a country ruled by Africans.

We arrived in Dar es Salaam the next day and I met Julius Nyerere, the newly independent country's first president. I reviewed our situation for him, ending with an appeal for help. He was a shrewd, soft-spoken man who was well disposed to our mission, but his perception of the situation surprised and dismayed me. He suggested we postpone the armed struggle until Sobukwe came out of prison. This was the first of many occasions when I learned of the PAC's appeal in the rest of Africa. I described the weakness of the PAC, and argued that a postponement would be a setback for the struggle as a whole. He suggested I seek the favour of Emperor Haile Selassie and promised to arrange an introduction.

I was meant to meet Oliver Tambo in Dar, but he left a message for me to follow him to Lagos, where he was to attend the Lagos Conference of Independent States. I had not seen Oliver for nearly two years, and when he met me at the airport in Accra I barely recognized him. Once clean-shaven and conservatively groomed, he now had a beard and wore military-style clothing. I complimented him on the tremendous work he had done abroad. He had already established ANC offices in Ghana, England, Egypt and Tanganyika, and had made valuable contacts for us in many other countries. Everywhere I subsequently travelled, I discovered the positive impression Oliver had made on diplomats and statesmen. He was the best possible ambassador for the organization.

The goal of the Lagos Conference of Independent States was to unite all African states, but it eventually disintegrated into bickering about which states to include or exclude. I kept a low profile and avoided the conference, for we did not want the South African government to know that I was abroad until I appeared at the PAFMECSA conference in Addis Ababa.

The conference in Ethiopia was officially opened by our host, His Imperial Majesty, who was dressed in an elaborate brocaded army uniform. I was scheduled to speak after the emperor, the only other speaker that morning. For the first time in many months, I flung aside the identity of David Motsamayi and became Nelson Mandela. In my speech, I reviewed the history of the freedom struggle in South Africa and listed the brutal massacres that had been committed against our people, from Bulhoek in 1921, when the army and police killed 183 unarmed peasants, to Sharpeville forty years later. I thanked the assembled nations for exerting pressure on South Africa, citing in particular Ghana, Nigeria and Tanganyika, who spearheaded the successful drive to oust South Africa from the British Commonwealth. I retraced the birth of Umkhonto we Sizwe, explaining that all opportunities for peaceful struggle had been closed to us.

The announcement that I would return to South Africa was met with loud cheers. We had been encouraged to speak first so that PAFMECSA could evaluate our cause and decide how much support to give it. There was a natural reluctance among many African states to support violent struggles elsewhere, but the speech persuaded people that freedom fighters in South Africa had no alternative but to take up arms.

Oliver and I had a private discussion with Kenneth Kaunda, the future president of Zambia. Like Julius Nyerere, Kaunda was worried about the lack of unity among South African freedom fighters and suggested that when Sobukwe emerged from jail, we might all join forces. Among Africans, the PAC had captured the spotlight at Sharpeville in a way that far exceeded their influence as an organization. Kaunda, who had once been a member of the ANC, told us he was concerned about our alliance with white communists and

With Oliver Tambo in Addis Ababa, 1962, where I spoke at the PAFMECSA conference. We had been encouraged to speak first so that the organization could evaluate our cause and decide how much support to give it. There was a natural reluctance among many African states to support violent struggles elsewhere, but the speech persuaded people that freedom fighters in South Africa had no alternative but to take up arms.

indicated that this reflected poorly on us in Africa. Communism was suspect not only in the West but in Africa. This came as something of a revelation to me, and it was a view that I was to hear over and over during my trip.

From Addis, Oliver, Robert Resha — who was to accompany me on the rest of my travels — and I flew to Cairo. Egypt was an important model for us, for we could witness at firsthand the programme of socialist economic reforms being launched by President Nasser. At that time, however, it was more important to us that Egypt was the only African state with an army, navy and air force that could in any way compare with those of South Africa.

After a day, Oliver left for London, promising to join Robbie and me in Ghana. In Tunis, our first stop, we met President Habib Bourguiba whose response was utterly positive and immediate: he offered training for our soldiers and £5,000 for weapons.

Rabat in Morocco, was our next stop. It was also the headquarters of the Algerian revolutionary army, and we spent several days with Dr Mustafa, head of the Algerian mission in Morocco, who briefed us on the history of the Algerian resistance to the French. The situation in Algeria was the closest model to our own in that the rebels faced a large white settler community that ruled the indigenous majority.

At first, the FLN believed they could defeat the French militarily, then realized that a purely military victory was impossible. Instead, they resorted to guerrilla warfare which was not designed to win a military victory so much as to unleash political and economic forces that would bring down the enemy. Dr Mustapha advised us not to neglect the political side of war while planning the military effort. International public opinion, he said, is sometimes worth more than a fleet of jet fighters.

From Morocco, I flew across the Sahara to Bamako, the capital of Mali, and then on to Guinea.

My next stop was Sierra Leone and then Liberia where I met President Tubman, who not only gave me $5,000 for weapons and training, but said in a quiet voice, 'Have you any pocket money?' I confessed that I was a bit low, and instantly an aide came back with an envelope containing $400 in cash. From Liberia, I went to Ghana, where I was met by Oliver and entertained by Guinea's resident minister, Abdoulaye Diallo. When I told him that I had not seen Sekou Touré in Guinea, he arranged for us to return immediately.

Oliver and I were impressed with Touré. We made our case to him, explained the history of the ANC and MK, and asked for $5,000 for the support of MK. He listened very carefully, and replied in a rather formal way. 'The government and the people of Guinea,' he said, as though giving a speech, 'fully support the struggle of our brothers in South Africa, and we have made statements at the UN to that effect.' He went to the bookcase, where he removed two books of his, which he autographed. He then said thank you, and we were dismissed.

Oliver and I were annoyed: we had wasted our time. A short while later, we were in our hotel room when an official from the Foreign Affairs Department knocked on our door

At Algerian Military Headquarters in Morocco, 1962. The situation in Algeria was the closest model to our own in that the rebels faced a large white settler community that ruled the indigenous majority. We visited an army unit at the front and at one point I took a pair of field glasses and could actually see French troops across the border. I confess I imagined I was looking at the uniforms of the South African Defence Force.

and presented us with a suitcase. It was filled with banknotes; Oliver and I looked at each other in glee. But then Oliver's expression changed. 'Nelson, this is Guinean currency,' he said. 'It is worthless outside here, just paper.' But Oliver had an idea: we took the money to the Czech embassy, where a friend exchanged it for a convertible currency.

In Dakar we met Senegalese President Léopold Senghor who did not then provide what we asked for, but furnished me with a diplomatic passport and paid for our plane fares from Dakar to our next destination: London.

I had several reasons for wanting to go to England, apart from my desire to see the country I had so long read about. I was concerned about Oliver's health and wanted to persuade him to receive treatment. I very much wanted to see Adelaide, his wife, and their children, as well as Yusuf Dadoo, who was now living there and representing the Congress movement. I also knew that in London I would be able to obtain literature on guerrilla warfare that I had been unable to acquire elsewhere.

In London, I resumed my old underground ways, not wanting word to leak back to South Africa that I was there. The tentacles of South African security forces reached all the way to London.

I had been informed by numerous people that the *Observer* newspaper, run by David Astor, had been tilting towards the PAC in its coverage, its editorials implying that the ANC was the party of the past. Oliver arranged for me to meet Astor at his house, and we talked at length about the ANC. I do not know if I had an effect on him, but the coverage certainly changed. He also recommended that I talk to a number of prominent politicians, and in the company of the Labour MP Denis Healey, I met Hugh Gaitskell, leader of the Labour Party, and Jo Grimond, leader of the Liberal Party.

It was only towards the end of my stay that I saw Yusuf, but it was not a happy reunion. Oliver and I had encountered a recurring difficulty in our travels: one African leader after another had questioned us about our relations with white and Indian communists, sometimes suggesting that they controlled the ANC. Our non-racialism would have been less of a problem had it not been for the formation of the explicitly nationalistic and anti-white PAC. In the rest of Africa, most African leaders could understand the views of the PAC better than those of the ANC. Oliver had discussed these things with Yusuf, who was unhappy about Oliver's conclusions. Oliver had resolved that the ANC had to appear more independent, taking certain actions unilaterally without the involvement of the other members of the Alliance, and I agreed.

I spent my last night in London discussing these issues with Yusuf. I explained that now that we were embarking on an armed struggle we would be relying on other African nations for money, training and support, and therefore had to take their views into account more than we did in the past. Yusuf believed that Oliver and I were changing ANC policy, that we were preparing to depart from the non-racialism that was the core of the Freedom Charter. I told him he was mistaken; we were not rejecting non-racialism; we were simply saying the ANC must stand more on its own and make statements that were not part of the Congress Alliance. Yusuf was unhappy about this. 'What about policy?' he kept asking. I told him I was not talking about policy, I was talking about image. We would still work together, only the ANC had to appear to be the first among equals.

Although I was sad to leave my friends in London, I was now embarking on what was to be the most unfamiliar part of my trip: military training. I had arranged to receive six months of training in Addis Ababa. My trainer was an experienced soldier, who had fought with the underground against the Italians. Our programme was strenuous: we trained from 8 a.m. until 1 p.m., broke for a shower and lunch, and then again from 2 to 4 p.m. From 4 p.m. into the evening I was lectured on military science by Colonel Tadesse, who was also assistant commissioner of police and had been instrumental in foiling a recent coup attempt against the emperor.

I learned how to use an automatic rifle and a pistol and took target practice both in Kolfe with the Emperor's Guard and at a shooting range about fifty miles away with the

London, 1962. My ten days in London were divided among ANC business, seeing old friends and occasional jaunts as a conventional tourist (opposite). With Mary Benson, a Pretoria-born friend who had written about our struggle, Oliver and I saw the sights of the city that had once commanded nearly two-thirds of the globe: Big Ben, the Houses of Parliament, Westminster Abbey (left). While I gloried in the beauty of these buildings, I was ambivalent about what they represented. When we saw the statue of General Smuts near Westminster Abbey, Oliver and I joked that perhaps some day there would be a statue of us in its stead.

entire battalion. I was taught about demolition and mortar-firing and I learned how to make small bombs and mines – and how to avoid them. I felt myself being moulded into a soldier and began to think as a soldier thinks – a far cry from the way a politician thinks.

The training course was meant to be six months long, but after eight weeks I received a telegram from the ANC urgently requesting that I return home. The internal armed struggle was escalating and they wanted the commander of MK on the scene. Colonel Tadesse rapidly arranged for me to take an Ethiopian flight to Khartoum and from there I went direct to Dar es Salaam, where I greeted the first group of Umkhonto recruits who were headed for Ethiopia to train as soldiers. It was a proud moment, for these men had volunteered for duty in an army I was then attempting to create. It was the first time that I was ever saluted by my own soldiers.

President Nyerere gave me a private plane to Mbeya, and I then flew directly to Kanye. From there we drove to Lobatse, where I met Joe Modise and an ANC supporter named Jonas Matlou. The local magistrate told me that the South African police were aware that I was returning, and suggested that I leave the next day. I thanked him for his help and advice, but when I arrived at Matlou's house, I said that I would leave that night. I was to drive back to South Africa with Cecil Williams, a white theatre director and member of MK. Posing as his chauffeur, I got behind the wheel and we left that night for Johannesburg.

Rivonia

After crossing the border, I breathed in deeply. The air of home always smells sweet after one has been away. We drove all night, reaching Liliesleaf Farm at dawn.

The following night we held a secret meeting for me to brief the Working Committee on my trip. Walter, Moses Kotane, Govan Mbeki, Dan Tloome, J.B. Marks and Duma Nokwe all arrived at the farm. I first gave a general overview of my travels, itemizing the money we had received and the offers of training. At the same time, I reported in detail the reservations I had encountered about the ANC's co-operation with whites, Indians and particularly communists. I proposed reshaping the Congress Alliance so that the ANC would clearly be seen as the leader, especially on issues directly affecting Africans.

This was a serious proposition, and the entire leadership had to be consulted. The Working Committee urged me to go down to Durban and brief Chief Luthuli.

I planned a series of secret meetings in Durban, the first with Monty Naicker and Ismail Meer to discuss the new proposal. Monty and Ismail were extremely close to the chief, and the chief trusted their views. I wanted to be able to tell Luthuli I had spoken to his friends and convey their reaction. Ismail and Monty, however, were disturbed by my belief that the ANC needed to take the lead among the Congress Alliance and make statements on its own concerning affairs that affected Africans.

I was taken to Groutville, where I explained the situation to the chief. He said he did not like the idea of foreign politicians dictating policy to the ANC. We had evolved the policy of non-racialism for good reasons and he did not think that we should alter our policy for a few foreign leaders. My plan, I told him, was simply to effect cosmetic changes in order to make the ANC more intelligible – and more palatable – to our allies.

The chief did not make decisions on the spur of the moment. I said farewell, and he advised me to be careful. I still had a number of clandestine meetings in the city and townships that evening. My last meeting was with the MK Regional Command in Durban.

Later that same evening, I was joined by Ismail and Fatima Meer, Monty Naicker, and J. N. Singh for a combination welcome-home and going-away party. It was a pleasant evening and my first night of relaxation in a long while. I met Cecil on Sunday afternoon – 5 August – for the long drive back to Johannesburg.

It was a clear, cool day and I revelled in the beauty of the Natal countryside. Cecil and I were engrossed in discussions as we passed through Howick, twenty miles northwest of Pietermaritzburg. At Cedara, a small town just past Howick, I noticed a Ford V-8 filled with white men shoot past us on the right. I instinctively turned round to look behind and saw two more cars filled with white men. Suddenly, in front of us, the Ford was signalling to us to stop. I knew in that instant that my life on the run was over.

When our car stopped, a tall man came over to the window. He introduced himself as Sergeant Vorster of the Pietermaritzburg police and produced an arrest warrant. He asked me to identify myself. I told him my name was David Motsamayi. He nodded, and then asked me a few questions about where I had been and where I was going. Then he said, 'Ag, you're Nelson Mandela, and this is Cecil Williams, and you are under arrest!'

I had always known that arrest was a possibility, but in my cell that night I realized I was not prepared for the reality of capture and confinement. I was upset and agitated. Someone had tipped the police off about my whereabouts. For weeks before my return, the police believed that I was already back in the country.

The authorities had been harassing Winnie in the belief that she would know whether I was back. I knew that they had followed her and searched the house on a number of occasions. I guessed they had figured I would visit Chief Luthuli directly upon my return, and they were correct. But I also suspected they had information that I was in Durban at that time. The movement had been infiltrated with informers, and even well-intentioned people were not as tight-lipped as they should have been. But such speculation is futile, and I soon fell asleep. At least on this night I did not have to worry about whether the police would find me.

In the morning I felt restored and braced myself for the new ordeal that lay ahead of me. I appeared before the local magistrate and was formally remanded to Johannesburg. The police had not taken elaborate security precautions and I merely sat in the back seat of a sedan, with two officers riding in front. Fatima Meer brought some food to the jail and I shared it with the two officers in the car.

But as we approached Johannesburg, the atmosphere changed. I was abruptly handcuffed, taken from the car, and placed in a sealed police van with windows reinforced with wire netting. The motorcade then took a circuitous route to Marshall Square as if they were concerned we might be ambushed.

I was planning my strategy for the next day, when I heard a cough from a nearby cell. There was something about this cough that struck me as curiously familiar. I sat up in sudden recognition: it was Walter. He had been arrested shortly me; we did not think that the arrests were unrelated.

The next day I appeared in court before a senior magistrate for formal remand. Harold Wolpe and Joe Slovo had come to court after hearing of my arrest, and we conferred in the basement. I had appeared before this magistrate on numerous occasions in my professional capacity and we had grown to respect one another. A number of attorneys were also present, some of whom I knew quite well. There I was, a fugitive, No. 1 on the state's Most Wanted list, a handcuffed outlaw who had been underground for more than a year, and yet the judge, the other attorneys and the spectators all greeted me with deference and professional courtesy. They knew me as Nelson Mandela, attorney at law, not Nelson Mandela, outlaw. It lifted my spirits immensely.

When I was asked the name of my counsel, I announced that I would represent myself, with Joe Slovo as legal adviser. By representing myself I would enhance the symbolism of my role. I would use my trial as a showcase for the ANC's moral opposition to racism. I listened silently to the charges: inciting African workers to strike and leaving the country without valid travel documents. In apartheid South Africa, the penalties for these 'crimes' could be as much as ten years in prison. Yet the charges were something of a relief: the state clearly did not have enough evidence to link me with Umkhonto we Sizwe or I would have been charged with the far more serious crimes of treason or sabotage.

From the court, I was taken to the Johannesburg Fort. When I emerged from the courthouse to enter the sealed van, there was a crowd of hundreds of people cheering and shouting 'Amandla!' followed by 'Ngawethu!' a popular ANC call-and-response meaning 'Power!' and 'The power is ours!'

I spent only a few days in the Fort before being transferred to Pretoria. In Johannesburg I had had a continuous stream of people coming to see me. I was now permitted visitors only twice a week. Despite the distance, Winnie came regularly and always brought clean clothes and delicious food. This was a way of showing her support, and every time I put on a fresh shirt I felt her love and devotion. I was aware of how difficult it must have been to get to Pretoria in the middle of the day in the middle of the week with two small children at home.

Through the prison grapevine, I learned that Walter had been brought to Pretoria as well, and although we were isolated from each other we did manage to communicate.

Walter had applied for bail — a decision I fully supported. He was simply too vital to the organization to be allowed to languish in jail.

Not long after I was transferred back to the Fort. A hearing had been set for October. Little can be said in favour of prison, but enforced isolation is conducive to study. I had begun correspondence studies for my LL B degree, which allows one to practise as an advocate.

There were two escape plans, one conceived by the ANC and communicated to me by Joe Slovo. I carefully considered it and concluded that it was premature, and the likelihood of failure unacceptably high. During a meeting with Joe, I passed him a note. MK was not ready for such an operation; even an elite force would probably not be able to accomplish such a mission. I suggested that it be postponed until I was a convicted prisoner and the authorities were less cautious. At the end, I wrote, 'Please destroy this.' Joe took my advice about the escape, but he decided the note should be saved as a historical document, and it later turned up at a very unfortunate time.

The initial hearing was set for Monday 15 October 1962. The organization had set up a Free Mandela Committee, which planned a mass demonstration at the courthouse. From press reports, I learned that a large and vociferous turnout was expected.
On Saturday, I was ordered to pack my things immediately: the hearing had been shifted to Pretoria. The authorities had made no announcement, and had I not managed to get word out through a sympathetic jailer, no one would have known. But the movement reacted quickly, and by the time my case began on Monday morning, the Old Synagogue was packed with supporters.

I entered the court that Monday morning wearing a traditional Xhosa leopard-skin *kaross* instead of a suit and tie. The crowd of supporters rose as one and with raised clenched fists shouted '*Amandla!*' and '*Ngawethu!*' The *kaross* electrified the spectators, some of whom had come all the way from the Transkei. Winnie also wore a traditional beaded headdress and an ankle-length Xhosa skirt.

I had chosen traditional dress to emphasize the symbolism that I was a black African walking into a white man's court. That day, I felt myself to be the embodiment of African nationalism, the inheritor of Africa's difficult but noble past and her uncertain future.

When the crowd had quietened down I immediately applied for a two-week remand on the grounds that I had been transferred to Pretoria without being given the opportunity of notifying my attorneys. I was granted a week's postponement.

When I was on my way back to my cell, a very nervous white warder said that the commanding officer, Colonel Jacobs, had ordered me to hand over the *kaross*. I refused and a short while later Colonel Jacobs himself appeared and ordered me to turn over my 'blanket'. I told him that he had no jurisdiction over the attire I chose to wear in court and if he tried to confiscate my *kaross* I would take the matter all the way to the Supreme Court.

During the trial the prosecutor called more than a hundred witnesses. Most of them gave technical evidence to show that I had left the country illegally and that I had incited

African workers to strike during the three-day stay-at-home in May 1961. It was indisputable that I was technically guilty of both charges.

Throughout the proceedings the prosecutor and the magistrate repeatedly inquired about the number of witnesses I intended to call. When the state finally concluded its case, there was a stillness in the courtroom in anticipation of the beginning of my defence. I rose and declared that I was not calling any witnesses at all, at which point I closed my case.

I had misled the court from the beginning because I knew the charge was accurate, and I saw no point in attempting to call witnesses and defend myself.

The following morning, the magistrate summed up the charges, after which I had my opportunity to speak. My plea in mitigation lasted over an hour. It was not a judicial appeal at all but a political testament. I wanted to explain to the court how and why I had become the man I was, why I had done what I had done, and why, if given the chance, I would do it again.

I enumerated the many times that we had brought our grievances before the government and the equal number of times that we were ignored. I described our stay-away of 1961 as a last resort after the government showed no signs of taking any steps to either talk with us or meet our demands. It was the government that provoked violence by employing violence to meet our non-violent demands. I explained that because of the government's actions we had taken a more militant stance. Whatever sentence the state imposed, it would do nothing to change my devotion to the struggle.

In a courtroom heavy with tension, the magistrate pronounced sentence: three years for inciting people to strike and two years for leaving the country without a passport; five years in all, with no possibility of parole. As the court rose, I turned to the gallery and again made a clenched fist, shouting '*Amandla!*' three times. Then, on its own, the crowd began to sing our anthem, '*Nkosi Sikelel' iAfrika*'. People sang and danced and the women ululated as I was led away. The uproar made me forget for a moment that I would be going to prison to serve what was then the stiffest sentence yet imposed in South Africa for a political offence.

I was stripped of my clothes and Colonel Jacobs was finally able to confiscate my *kaross*. I was issued the standard prison uniform for Africans: a pair of short trousers, a rough khaki shirt, a canvas jacket, socks, sandals and a cloth cap.

I informed the authorities that I would under no circumstances wear shorts and told them I was prepared to go to court to protest. Later, when I was brought dinner, stiff cold porridge with half a teaspoonful of sugar, I refused to eat it. Colonel Jacobs came up with a solution: I could wear long trousers and have my own food, if I agreed to be put in isolation. 'We were going to put you with the other politicals,' he said, 'but now you will be alone, man. I hope you enjoy it.' I assured him that solitary confinement would be fine as long as I could wear and eat what I chose.

For the next few weeks, I was completely and utterly isolated. I was locked up for twenty-three hours a day, with thirty minutes of exercise in the morning and again in the

❛I was made, by the law, a criminal, not because of what I had done, but because of what I stood for, because of what I thought, because of my conscience. Can it be any wonder to anybody that such conditions make a man an outlaw of society?❜

afternoon. I had never been in isolation before, and every hour seemed like a year. There was no natural light in my cell; a single bulb burned overhead twenty-four hours a day. I did not have a wristwatch and I often thought it was the middle of the night when it was only late afternoon. I had nothing to read, nothing to write on or with, no one to talk to.

After a few weeks I was ready to swallow my pride and tell Colonel Jacobs that I would trade my long trousers for some company. I demanded to be put with the other political prisoners at Pretoria Local. Among them was Robert Sobukwe. My request was ultimately granted. I don't think I ever looked forward to eating cold mealie pap so much in my life.

Apart from my desire for company, I was keen to talk with Sobukwe and the others, most of whom were PAC, because I thought that in prison we might forge a unity that we could not on the outside.

When I was taken to the courtyard with the others, we greeted each other warmly. Robert asked me to give an account of my African tour, which I did gladly. I was candid about how both the PAC and the ANC were perceived in the rest of Africa. At the end of my narrative I said there were issues that I wanted us to examine. But after initially allowing Sobukwe and me a certain proximity, the authorities took pains to keep us apart.

We were joined for two weeks by Walter Sisulu, who had been on trial in Johannesburg for incitement to strike while I had been in Pretoria. He was sentenced to six years. We had a number of opportunities to talk in jail and we discussed Walter's application for bail while his appeal was pending. After two weeks he was released on bail, and he was instructed by the movement to go underground, from where he was to continue to lead the struggle, which he ably did.

One night towards the end of May, a warder came to my cell and ordered me to pack my things. In less than ten minutes, I was escorted down to the reception office where I found three other political prisoners: Tefu, John Gaetsewe and Aaron Molete. Colonel Aucamp curtly informed us that we were being transferred. Where? Tefu asked. Someplace very beautiful, Aucamp said. 'Where?' said Tefu. '*Die Eiland*' said Aucamp. The island. There was only one. Robben Island.

The four of us were shackled together and put in a windowless van that contained only a sanitary bucket. We drove all night to Cape Town, and arrived at the city's docks in the late afternoon.

The docks at Cape Town were swarming with armed police and nervous plain-clothed officials. We had to stand, still chained, in the hold of the old wooden ferry, which was difficult as the ship rocked in the swells off the coast. A small porthole above was the only source of light and air. The porthole served another purpose as well: the warders enjoyed urinating on us from above. It was still light when we were led on deck and we saw the island for the first time. Green and beautiful, it looked at first more like a resort than a prison.

We were met by a group of burly white warders shouting: '*Dis die Eiland! Hier gaan julle vrek!* ('This is the island. Here you will die!') Ahead of us was a compound flanked by a number of guardhouses. Armed guards lined the path to the compound. It was extremely tense. A tall, red-faced warder yelled at us: '*Hier is ek you baas!*' 'Here I am your boss!' He was one of the notorious Kleynhans brothers, known for their brutality to prisoners.

We were taken to a large open room, the floor covered with water a few inches deep. The guards yelled: '*Trek uit! Trek uit!*' ('Undress! Undress!') As we removed each item of clothing, the guards would grab it, search it quickly and then throw it in the water. Jacket off, searched, thrown in the water. Then the guards commanded us to get dressed, by which they meant for us to put on our soaking clothes.

We were then taken to our cell, one of the best I had ever seen. It was spacious, certainly large enough for the four of us, and had its own toilets and showers. It had been an exhausting day and a short while later, after a supper of cold porridge, we went to sleep.

One day a captain came to our cell and commanded the four of us to pack our belongings. Within minutes my comrades were taken away, leaving me in the cell by myself. Very early the next morning I was taken back to Pretoria. The Department of Prisons released a statement to the press that I had been removed from the island for my own safety because PAC prisoners were planning to assault me.

I was kept in solitary confinement at Pretoria Local. But prisoners are resourceful and I was soon receiving secret notes and other communications from some of the ANC people there. I had a communication from Henry Fazzie, one of the MK cadres who had undergone military training in Ethiopia and been arrested while attempting to return to South Africa. They were among the first ANC members to be tried under the Sabotage Act.

Through the prison grapevine, I attempted to help them with their defence and suggested they contact Harold Wolpe. I later heard that Wolpe was in police detention. This was my first intimation that something had gone seriously wrong. One day, as I was being led away from the courtyard after exercise, I saw Andrew Mlangeni. I had last seen him in September 1961 when he was leaving the country for military training. Wolpe, Mlangeni – who else was under arrest?

Early in 1961, Winnie had been banned for two years. I heard from another prisoner that Winnie had recently been charged with violating her bans, which could lead to imprisonment or house arrest. I had no doubt that she violated her orders, and I would never counsel her not to do so, but it concerned me greatly that she might spend time in prison.

One morning in July 1963, as I was walking along the corridor to my cell, I saw Thomas Mashifane, who had been the foreman at Liliesleaf Farm. His presence there could mean only one thing: the authorities had discovered Rivonia.

A day or two later I was summoned to the prison office where I found Walter; Govan Mbeki; Ahmed Kathrada; Andrew Mlangeni; Bob Hepple; Raymond Mhlaba, a member of the MK High Command who had recently returned from training in China; Elias

The raid by the police
on the 'safe house'
at Liliesleaf Farm, Rivonia,
on 11 July 1963, was
a coup for the state.

Motsoaledi, also a member of MK; Dennis Goldberg, an engineer and a member of the Congress of Democrats; Rusty Bernstein, an architect and also a member of the COD; and Jimmy Kantor, an attorney who was Harold Wolpe's brother-in-law. We were all charged with sabotage, and scheduled to appear in court the next day.

I gradually learned what had happened. On the afternoon of 11 July, a van drove up to the farm and dozens of armed policemen and several police dogs sprang out. They surrounded the property and entered the main building. The police confiscated hundreds of documents and papers, though they found no weapons. One of the most important documents was Operation Mayibuye, a plan for guerrilla warfare in South Africa. In one fell swoop, the police had captured the entire High Command of Umkhonto we Sizwe. Everyone was detained under the new Ninety-Day Detention Law. The raid was a coup for the state.

We were brought before a magistrate and charged with sabotage. A few days later we were allowed to meet Bram, Vernon Berrangé, Joel Joffe, George Bizos and Arthur Chaskalson, all of whom were acting for us. I was still being kept separately as I was a convicted prisoner, and these sessions were my first opportunity to talk with my colleagues.

Bram was very sombre. He told us that the state had formally advised him they would ask for the supreme penalty permitted by law, the death sentence. Given the climate of the times, Bram said, this was a very real possibility. From that moment on we lived in the shadow of the gallows. The mere possibility of a death sentence changes everything. From the start, we considered it the most likely outcome of the trial. Far lesser crimes than ours had recently been punished by life sentences.

On 9 October 1963, we were driven to the Palace of Justice in Pretoria for the opening of 'The State versus the National High Command and others', better known as the Rivonia Trial.

The Palace of Justice was teeming with armed policemen. All around the building police officers with machine guns stood at attention. As we got out, we could hear the great crowd singing and chanting.

When we entered the courtroom, we each turned to the crowd and made a clenched-fist ANC salute. In the visitors' gallery our supporters shouted 'Amandla! Ngawethu!' and 'Mayibuye Afrika!' This was inspiring, but dangerous: the police took the names and addresses of all the spectators in the galleries, and photographed them as they left the court. The courtroom was filled with domestic and international journalists, and dozens of representatives of foreign governments.

Our judge in the Rivonia Trial, Mr Quartus de Wet, judge-president of the Transvaal, was one of the last judges appointed by the United Party before the Nationalists came to power, and was not considered a government lackey. The prosecutor was Dr Percy Yutar, deputy attorney general of the Transvaal, whose ambition was to become attorney general of South Africa.

We were charged with sabotage and conspiracy rather than high treason because the law does not require a long preparatory examination (which is highly useful to the defence) for sabotage and conspiracy. Yet the supreme penalty – death by hanging – is the same. With high treason, the state must prove its case beyond a reasonable doubt; under the Sabotage Law, the onus was on the defence to prove the accused innocent.

Bram Fischer stood up and asked the court for a remand on the grounds that the defence had not had time to prepare its case. He noted that a number of the accused had been held in solitary confinement for unconscionable lengths of time. The state had been preparing for three months, but we had only received the indictment that day. Justice de Wet gave us a three-week adjournment until 29 October.

On 29 October, we again entered the Palace of Justice; again the crowds were large and excited; again the court was filled with dignitaries from many foreign embassies.

We went on the attack immediately – Bram Fischer criticized the state's indictment as shoddy, poorly drawn and containing absurdities such as the allegation that I had participated in certain acts of sabotage on dates when I was in Pretoria Local. Yutar was flummoxed. De Wet was impatient with Yutar's fumbling and told him so. He then quashed the indictment.

For that moment we were technically free, and there was pandemonium in the court. But we were rearrested even before Judge de Wet left his seat. Lieutenant Swanepoel clapped each of us on the shoulder and said, 'I am arresting you on a charge of sabotage', and we were herded back to our cells. Even so, this was a blow to the government, for it now had to go back to the drawing-board in the case it was calling the trial to end all trials.

The state redrew its indictment and we were back in court in early December. The new charges were read: we were alleged to have recruited persons for sabotage and guerrilla warfare for the purpose of starting a violent revolution; we had allegedly conspired to aid foreign military units to invade the republic in order to support a communist revolution; and we had solicited and received funds from foreign countries for this purpose.

Yutar argued that from the time the ANC had been driven underground, the organization had embarked on a policy of violence designed to lead from sabotage through guerrilla warfare to an armed invasion of the country. He asserted that we planned to deploy thousands of trained guerrilla units throughout the country, and these units were to spearhead an uprising that would be followed by an armed invasion by military units of a foreign power.

We wondered what evidence the state had to prove my guilt. I had been out of the

The trial made front page headlines all over the country (right). My plea in mitigation lasted over an hour. It was not a judicial appeal at all but a political testament. I wanted to explain to the court how and why I had become the man I was, why I had done what I had done, and why, if given the chance, I would do it again.

Because of her banning and her restriction to Johannesburg, Winnie needed police permission to come to court. She had applied and been refused. She subsequently appealed to the minister of justice, who granted her permission to attend the trial on condition that she did not wear traditional dress.

country and in prison while much of the planning at Rivonia had taken place. When I saw Walter in Pretoria Local, I urged him to make sure that all my books and notes were removed from the farm. But during the first week of the trial, when Rusty Bernstein applied for bail, Percy Yutar dramatically produced the sketch of the Fort and the accompanying note about escape that I had made while detained there. Yutar exclaimed that this was evidence that all of the accused meant to escape. It was a sign that nothing of mine had been removed from Rivonia. Later, I was told that my colleagues at Rivonia had decided to preserve my escape note because they thought it would be historic in the future. But in the present, it cost Rusty Bernstein his bail.

The keystone of the state's case was the six-page Plan of Action confiscated in the Rivonia raid. Operation Mayibuye sketches out in general form the plan for the possible commencement of guerrilla operations, and how it might spark a mass armed uprising against the government. It envisions an initial landing of small guerrilla forces in four different areas of South Africa and the attacking of preselected targets. The document set a goal of some 7,000 MK recruits in the country who would meet the initial outside force of 120 trained guerrillas.

The prosecution's case rested in large part on their contention that Operation Mayibuye had been approved by the ANC Executive and had become the operating plan of MK. We insisted that Operation Mayibuye had not yet been formally adopted and was still under discussion at the time of the arrests. As far as I was concerned, it was a draft document that was not only not approved, but was entirely unrealistic in its goals and plans.

The plan had been drafted in my absence, so I had very little knowledge of it. Even among the Rivonia Trialists there was disagreement as to whether the plan had been adopted as ANC policy. Govan, who had drafted the document with Joe Slovo, insisted that it had been agreed upon. But all the other accused contended that the document, while drawn up by the High Command, had not been approved by the ANC Executive or even seen by Chief Luthuli.

The state case continued during the Christmas season of 1963, ending on 29 February 1964. We had a little over a month to examine the evidence and prepare our defence. There was no evidence against James Kantor; he was not even a member of our organization and should not have been on trial at all. For Rusty Bernstein, Raymond Mhlaba and Ahmed Kathrada, the evidence of involvement in conspiracy was slight and we decided they should not incriminate themselves. In Rusty's case, the evidence was negligible; he had merely been found at Rivonia with the others. The remaining six of us would make admissions of guilt on certain charges.

Bram was deeply pessimistic. Even if we proved that guerrilla war had not been approved and our policy of sabotage was designed not to sacrifice human life, the state could still impose the death sentence. The defence team was divided on whether or not we should testify. George Bizos, though, suggested that unless we gave evidence and convinced the judge that we had not decided on guerrilla warfare, he would certainly impose the supreme penalty.

I would be the first witness and therefore set the tone for the defence. We decided that instead of giving testimony, I would read a statement from the dock, while the others would testify and go through cross-examination.

I spent about a fortnight drafting my address. I asked Bram Fischer to look it over. Bram became concerned and got a respected advocate named Hal Hanson to read it. Hanson told Bram, 'If Mandela reads this in court they will take him straight out to the back of the courthouse and string him up.' Bram begged me not to read the final paragraph, but I was adamant.

On Monday 20 April, under the tightest of security, we were taken to the Palace of Justice, this time to begin our defence. Winnie was there with my mother, and I nodded to them as we entered the court, which was again full.

Bram announced that certain parts of the state's evidence would be conceded by the accused, and there was a buzz in the court. But he went on to say that the defence would deny a number of the state's assertions, including the contention that Umkhonto we Sizwe was the military wing of the ANC. He stated that the defence would show that Umkhonto had not in fact adopted Operation Mayibuye, and that MK had not embarked on preparations for guerrilla warfare.

'Then Bram said, 'The defence case, My Lord, will commence with a statement from the dock by accused No. 1, who personally took part in the establishment of Umkhonto, and who will be able to inform the court of the beginnings of that organization.'

I rose and faced the courtroom and read slowly.

After I had finished, the silence in the courtroom was complete. I had read for over four hours. It was a little after 4 in the afternoon, the time court normally adjourned. But Justice de Wet, as soon as there was order in the courtroom, asked for the next witness. He was determined to lessen the impact of my statement, but nothing he did could weaken its effect.

The speech received wide publicity in both the local and foreign press, and was printed, virtually word for word, in the *Rand Daily Mail*. This despite the fact that all my words were banned. The speech both indicated our line of defence and disarmed the prosecution, which had prepared its entire case based on the expectation that I would be denying responsibility for sabotage. It was now plain that we would not attempt to use legal

niceties to avoid accepting responsibility for actions we had taken with pride and premeditation.

Accused No. 2, Walter Sisulu, was next. Walter withstood a barrage of hostile questions to explain our policy in clear and simple terms. He asserted that Operation Mayibuye and the policy of guerrilla warfare had not been adopted as ANC policy. In fact, Walter told the court that he had personally opposed its adoption on the grounds that it was premature.

Govan, Ahmed Kathrada and Rusty Bernstein testified to their membership of the Communist Party as well as the ANC. Although Rusty was captured at Rivonia during the raid, the only direct evidence that the state had against him was that he had assisted in the erection of a radio aerial at the farm. Kathy, in his sharp-witted testimony, denied committing acts of sabotage or inciting others to do so, but he said he supported such acts if they advanced the struggle.

Raymond Mhlaba was one of the leading ANC and MK figures in the eastern Cape, but because the state did not have much evidence against him, he denied he was a member of MK and that he knew anything about sabotage. The defence rested. All that remained were the final arguments and then judgment.

Defence counsel Arthur Chaskalson rose first to deal with some of the legal questions raised by the prosecution. He rejected Yutar's statement that the trial had anything to do with murder, and reminded the court that MK's express policy was that there should be no loss of life. When Arthur began to explain that other organizations committed acts of sabotage for which the accused were blamed, de Wet interrupted to say he already accepted that as a fact. This was another unexpected victory.

Bram Fischer spoke next and was prepared to tackle the state's two most serious contentions: that we had undertaken guerrilla warfare and that the ANC and MK were the same. Though de Wet had said he believed that guerrilla warfare had not yet begun, we were taking no chances. But as Bram launched into his first point, de Wet interjected somewhat testily, 'I thought I made my attitude clear. I accept that no decision or date was fixed upon for guerrilla warfare.'

When Bram began his second point, de Wet again interrupted him to say that he also conceded the fact that the two organizations were separate. Bram, who was usually prepared for anything, was hardly prepared for de Wet's response. He then sat down; the judge had accepted his arguments even before he had made them. We were jubilant – that is, if men facing the death sentence can be said to be jubilant. Court was adjourned for three weeks while de Wet considered the verdict.

On Thursday 11 June we reassembled in the Palace of Justice for the verdict. We knew that for at least six of us there could be no verdict but guilty. The question was the sentence.

De Wet pronounced each of the main accused guilty on all counts. Kathy was found guilty on only one of four counts, and Rusty Bernstein was found not guilty and discharged.

'I do not propose to deal with the question of sentence today,' de Wet said. 'The state and the defence will be given opportunities to make any submission they want tomorrow morning at ten o'clock.' Court was then adjourned.

We had hoped that Kathy and Mhlaba might escape conviction, but it was another sign, if one was necessary, that the state was taking a harsh line. If he could convict Mhlaba on all four counts with little evidence, could the death sentence be far behind for those of us against whom the evidence was overwhelming?

That night, after a discussion among ourselves, Walter, Govan and I informed counsel that whatever sentences we received, even the death sentence, we would not appeal. Our decision stunned our lawyers. Walter, Govan and I believed an appeal would undermine the moral stance we had taken. We had from the first maintained that what we had done, we had done proudly and for moral reasons. We were not going to suggest otherwise in an appeal. If a death sentence was passed, we did not want to hamper the mass campaign that would surely spring up. Our message was that no sacrifice was too great in the struggle for freedom.

I was prepared for the death penalty. To be truly prepared for something, one must actually expect it. We were all prepared, not because we were brave but because we were realistic. I thought of the line from Shakespeare: 'Be absolute for death; for either death or life shall be the sweeter.'

On Friday 12 June 1964 we entered court for the last time. Nearly a year had passed since the fateful arrests at Rivonia. Security was extraordinarily high.

Before sentence was passed, there were two pleas in mitigation. One was delivered by Harold Hanson and the other by the author Alan Paton, who was also national president of the Liberal Party. Hanson spoke eloquently, saying that a nation's grievances cannot be suppressed, that people will always find a way to give voice to those grievances.

Though Paton did not himself support violence, he said the accused had had only two alternatives: 'to bow their heads and submit, or to resist by force'. The defendants should receive clemency, he said, otherwise the future of South Africa would be bleak.

But de Wet seemed absorbed in his own thoughts. He nodded for us to rise. His face was very pale, and he was breathing heavily. We looked at each other and seemed to know: it would be death, otherwise why was this normally calm man so nervous? And then he began to speak.

> The function of this court, as is the function of the court in any other country, is to enforce law and order and to enforce the laws of the state within which it functions. The crime of which the accused have been convicted, that is the main crime, the crime of conspiracy, is in essence one of high treason. The state has decided not to charge the crime in this form. Bearing this in mind and giving the matter very serious consideration I have decided not to impose the supreme penalty which in a case like this would usually be the proper penalty for the crime, but consistent with my duty that is the only leniency which I can show. The sentence in the case of all the accused will be one of life imprisonment.

The police were extremely nervous about the crowd outside. They kept us underground for more than half an hour, hoping people would disperse. We were taken through the back of the building and entered the black van. To avoid the crowd, the van took a different route, but even so, we could hear the crowd shouting '*Amandla!*', and the slow beautiful rhythms of '*Nkosi Sikelel' iAfrika*'.

That night, I ran over the reasons for de Wet's decision. The demonstrations throughout South Africa and the international pressure undoubtedly weighed on his mind. International trade unions had protested. Dock-workers' unions around the world threatened not to handle South African goods. The Russian prime minister, Leonid Brezhnev, wrote to Dr Verwoerd asking for leniency. Members of the United States

Congress protested. Fifty members of the British Parliament had staged a march in London. Alec Douglas-Home, the British foreign secretary, was rumoured to be working behind the scenes to help our cause. Adlai Stevenson, the US representative at the UN, wrote a letter saying that his government would do everything it could to prevent a death sentence. I thought that once de Wet had accepted that we had not yet initiated guerrilla warfare and that the ANC and MK were separate entities, it would have been difficult to impose the death penalty; it would have seemed excessive.

Verwoerd told Parliament that the judgment had not been influenced by the telegrams of protest and representations that had come in from around the world. He boasted that he had tossed into the waste-basket all the telegrams from socialist nations.

Every evening, in Pretoria Local, before lights were out, the jail would echo to African prisoners singing freedom songs. We too would sing in this great swelling chorus. But, each evening, seconds before the lights were dimmed, as if in obedience to some silent command, the hum of voices would stop and the entire jail would become silent. Then, from a dozen places throughout the prison, men would yell '*Amandla!*' This would be met by hundreds of voices replying '*Ngawethu!*'

There had been a great collective gasp in the courtroom when de Wet announced that he was not sentencing us to death. I turned and smiled broadly to the gallery, searching out Winnie's face and that of my mother, but it was extremely confused in the court, with people shouting. I could not see them. Our police guardians began to hustle us out of the dock and towards the door leading underground, but although I looked again for Winnie's face, I was not able to see her before I ducked through the door leading to the cells below.

Robben Island: The Dark Years

I was assigned a cell at the head of the corridor. It overlooked the courtyard and had a small eye-level window. I could walk the length of my cell in three paces. When I lay down, I could feel the wall with my feet and my head grazed the concrete at the other side. The width was about six feet, and the walls were at least two feet thick. I was forty-six years old, a political prisoner with a life sentence, and that small cramped space was to be my home for I knew not how long.

At midnight, I was awake and staring at the ceiling – images from the trial were still rattling around in my head when I heard steps coming down the corridor. There was a knock at my door and I could see Colonel Aucamp's face at the bars.

'You are a lucky man,' he said. 'We are taking you to a place where you will have your freedom. You will be able to move around; you'll see the ocean and the sky, not just grey walls.'

He intended no sarcasm, but I well knew that the place he was referring to would not afford me the freedom I longed for. He then remarked rather cryptically, 'As long as you don't make trouble, you'll get everything you want.'

Aucamp then woke the others and ordered them to pack their things. Fifteen minutes later we were making our way through the iron labyrinth of Pretoria Local, with its endless series of clanging metal doors echoing in our ears.

We landed at an airstrip on one end of the island. It was a grim, overcast day, and when I stepped out of the plane, the cold winter wind whipped through our thin prison uniforms. We were met by guards with automatic weapons; the atmosphere was tense but quiet, unlike the boisterous reception I had received two years before.

A return trip to the cell (above).

We were driven to the old jail, an isolated stone building, where we were ordered to strip while standing outside. One of the ritual indignities of prison life is that when you are transferred from one prison to another, the first thing that happens is that you change from the garb of the old prison to that of the new. When we were undressed, we were thrown the plain khaki uniforms of Robben Island.

One morning the front gate swung open to reveal the commanding officer with a reporter and photographer from the *Daily Telegraph* in London. We well knew that there was great concern in the outside world about our situation and that it was in the government's interest to show that we were not being mistreated. I talked to the reporter for about twenty minutes, and was candid about both prison and the Rivonia Trial.

I was reluctant to be photographed, but relented because I knew the photograph would be published only overseas, and might serve to help our cause. I told him I would agree, provided Mr Sisulu could join me.

The warders pointed with their guns to where they wanted us to go, and barked their orders in simple one-word commands: 'Move!' 'Silence!' 'Halt!' They did not threaten us in the swaggering way that I recalled from my previous stay, and betrayed no emotion.

The fourth morning we were handcuffed and taken in a covered truck to a prison within a prison. This new structure was a one-storey rectangular stone fortress with a flat cement courtyard in the centre, about one hundred feet by thirty feet. It had cells on three of the four sides. The fourth side was a twenty-foot-high wall with a catwalk patrolled by guards with German shepherds. We were each given individual cells on either side of a long corridor, with half the cells facing the courtyard. There were about thirty cells in all. Each cell had one window, about a foot square, covered with iron bars.

That first week we began the work that would occupy us for the next few months. Each morning, a load of stones was dumped by the entrance to the courtyard. Using wheelbarrows, we moved the stones to the centre of the yard. We were given either four-pound hammers, or fourteen-pound hammers for the larger stones. Our job was to crush the stones into gravel.

Warders walked among us to enforce the silence. During those first few weeks, warders from other sections and even other prisons came to stare at us as if we were a collection of rare caged animals. The work was tedious and difficult; it was not strenuous enough to keep us warm but demanding enough to make all our muscles ache.

June and July were the bleakest months on Robben Island. Winter was in the air, and the rains were just beginning. Even in the sun, I shivered in my light khaki shirt. At noon we would break for lunch. That first week all we were given was soup, which stank horribly. In the afternoons we were permitted to exercise for half an hour under strict supervision. We walked briskly around the courtyard in single file.

Robben Island had changed since I had been there in 1962. Then, there were few prisoners; the place seemed more like an experiment than a fully-fledged prison. Two years later, Robben Island was without question the harshest, most iron-fisted outpost in the South African penal system. It was a hardship station not only for the prisoners but for the prison staff. The warders, white and overwhelmingly Afrikaans-speaking, demanded a master-servant relationship. The racial divide on Robben Island was absolute: there were no black warders, and no white prisoners.

At the end of our first two weeks on the island, we were informed that our lawyers, Bram Fischer and Joel Joffe, were going to be visiting to see how we had settled in, and to verify that we still did not want to appeal. It had only been a few weeks since I had seen them, but it felt like an eternity. They seemed like visitors from another world.

Our job was to crush the stones into gravel. We were divided into four rows, about a yard-and-a-half apart, and sat cross-legged on the ground. We were each given a thick rubber ring, made from tyres, in which to place the stones. The ring was meant to catch flying chips of stone, but hardly ever did so. We wore makeshift wire masks to protect our eyes. Other prisoners sat in rows sewing mailbags.

On the morning of the *Telegraph* visit the warders, instead of handing us hammers, gave us each needles and thread and a pile of worn prison jerseys to repair (below). We wondered what had provoked the change – until the arrival of the reporters. After they had gone the warders removed the jerseys and gave us back our hammers.

I explained that we were still opposed to an appeal for all the reasons we had previously enunciated, including the fact that we did not want our appeal to interfere with the cases of other ANC defendants. Bram and Joel seemed resigned to this, though I knew Bram believed we should mount an appeal.

Within a few months our life settled into a pattern. Prison life is about routine: each day like the one before; each week like the one before it, so that the months and years blend into each other. Anything that departs from this pattern upsets the authorities, for routine is the sign of a well-run prison.

Watches and timepieces of any kind were barred on Robben Island, so we never knew precisely what time it was. We were dependent on bells and warders' whistles and shouts. One of the first things I did was to make a calendar on the wall of my cell. Losing a sense of time is an easy way to lose one's grip and even one's sanity.

The challenge for every prisoner, particularly every political prisoner, is how to survive prison intact, how to emerge from prison undiminished, how to conserve one's beliefs. I do not know that I could have done it had I been alone. But the authorities' greatest mistake was to keep us together, for together our determination was reinforced. We supported each other and gained strength from each other. Men react differently to stress. But the stronger ones raised up the weaker ones, and both became stronger in the process.

I never thought that a life sentence truly meant life and that I would die behind bars. Perhaps I was denying this prospect because it was too unpleasant to contemplate. But I always knew that someday I would once again feel the grass under my feet and walk in the sunshine as a free man.

In jail, all prisoners are classified by the authorities as one of four categories: A, B, C or D. A is the highest classification and confers the most privileges; D is the lowest and confers the least. All political prisoners were automatically classified as D on admission. The privileges affected by these classifications included visits and letters, studies, and the opportunity to buy groceries and incidentals. It normally took years for a political prisoner to raise his status from D to C.

As a D group prisoner, I was entitled to have only one visitor, and write and receive only one letter every six months. I found this one of the most inhumane restrictions of the prison system. Communication with one's family is a human right; it should not be restricted by the artificial gradations of a prison system.

The anticipation of mail was overwhelming. Mail-call took place once a month, and sometimes six months would go by without a letter. Often the authorities would withhold mail out of spite. I can remember warders saying, 'Mandela, we have received a letter for you, but we cannot give it to you.' No explanation of why, or who the letter is from.

When letters did arrive, they were cherished. A letter was like the summer rain that could make even the desert bloom. When I was handed a letter by the authorities, I would not rush forward and grab it as I felt like doing, but take it in a leisurely manner. I would not give the authorities the satisfaction of seeing my eagerness. During

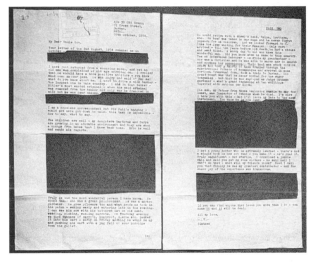

the first few months, I received one letter from Winnie, but it was so heavily censored that not much more than the salutation was left.

At the end of August, after I had been on the island less than three months, I was informed by the authorities that I would have a visitor the following day. They would not tell me who it was. Walter was informed that he, too, would have a visitor, and I hoped that it would be a visit from Winnie and Albertina.

From the moment Winnie learned we had been brought to the island, she had been trying to arrange a visit. As a banned person, she had to receive a special dispensation from the minister of justice, for she was technically not permitted to communicate with me.

Visiting Robben Island was not an easy proposition. Visits were a maximum of thirty minutes long, and political prisoners were not permitted contact visits, in which the visitor and prisoner were in the same room.

The visiting room was cramped and windowless. On the prisoner's side was a row of five cubicles with small square pieces of glass that looked out on identical cubicles on the other side. One sat in a chair and looked through the thick, smudged glass that had a few small holes drilled into it to permit conversation. One had to talk very loudly to be heard.

Visits did not seem to be planned in advance by the authorities. One day, they would contact your wife and say, 'You have permission to visit your husband tomorrow.' This was enormously inconvenient, and often had the effect of making visits impossible. If a family member was able to plan a visit in advance, the authorities would sometimes deliberately delay issuing a permit until after the plane had departed. Since most of the men's families lived far from the Cape and had very little money, visits by family members were often far beyond their means. I knew of men who spent a decade or more on Robben Island without a single visit.

Walter and I were called to the visitors' office in the late morning and took seats at the far end of the room. I waited with some anxiety, and suddenly on the other side of the window was Winnie's lovely face. Winnie always dressed up for prison visits, and tried to wear something new and elegant. It was tremendously frustrating not to be able to touch my wife, to speak tenderly to her, to have a private moment together.

I could see immediately that Winnie was under tremendous strain. Just getting to the island itself was difficult, and added to that were the harsh rituals of the prison, the undoubted indignities of the warders and the impersonality of the contact. Winnie, I later discovered, had recently received a second banning order and had been dismissed from her job at the Child Welfare Office as a result. Her office was searched by the police shortly before she was sacked. The authorities were convinced that she was in secret communication with me. Winnie loved her job as a social worker. It was the hands-on end of the struggle: placing babies with adoptive parents, finding work for the unemployed and medical help for the uninsured. The banning and harassment of my wife greatly troubled me: I could not look after her and the children, and the state was making it difficult for her to look after herself. My powerlessness gnawed at me.

Walter Sisulu and his wife re-enact a visit (above) on a trip back to Robben Island.

Our conversation was awkward at first, and was not made easier by the presence of two warders standing directly behind her and three behind me. Their role was not only to monitor but to intimidate. Regulations dictated that conversation had to be in either English or Afrikaans and could involve family matters only. Any line of talk that verged on the political might mean the abrupt termination of the visit. If a name was unfamiliar to the warders, they would interrupt the conversation, and ask who the person was and the nature of the relationship. But their ignorance also worked in our favour: it allowed us to invent code names for people we wanted to talk about.

I inquired one by one about all the children, about my mother and sisters and Winnie's own family. Suddenly, I heard the warder say, 'Time up! Time up!' I turned and looked at him with incredulity. It was impossible that half an hour had passed. Winnie and I were hustled from our chairs and we waved a quick farewell. Over the next days, weeks and months, I would return to that one visit again and again. I knew I would not be able to see my wife again for at least six months. As it turned out, Winnie was not able to visit me for another two years.

One morning in early January, as we lined up to be counted before beginning work in the courtyard, we were instead marched outside and ordered into a covered truck. It was the first time that we had left our compound. A few minutes later we emerged from the truck in a place that I had first seen when I was on the island in 1962: the lime quarry.

We were met by the commanding officer, Colonel Wessels. We stood at attention as he told us that the work we would be doing would last six months and afterwards we would be given light tasks for the duration of our terms. His timing was considerably off. We remained at the quarry for the next thirteen years.

The lime quarry looked like an enormous white crater cut into a rocky hillside. After arriving in the morning, we would fetch our picks, shovels, hammers and wheelbarrows from a zinc shed. Then we would assemble along the quarry face, usually in groups of three or four. Warders with automatic weapons stood on raised platforms watching us. Unarmed warders walked among us, urging us to work harder. Go on! Go on!, they would shout, as if we were oxen. By eleven, when the sun was high in the sky, we would begin to flag. By that time I would already be drenched in sweat. At midday, a whistle would blow, and we would make our way to the bottom of the hill. We sat on makeshift seats under a simple zinc shed shielding us from the sun and drums of boiled mealies were delivered to us. We worked until four, when we carted the lime to the waiting truck. By the end of the day, our faces and bodies were caked with white dust. We looked like pale ghosts except where rivulets of sweat had washed away the lime.

We were joined by a number of other prominent political prisoners. Eddie Daniels (below left) was a Coloured member of the Liberal Party who had been convicted of sabotage. Eddie was to become one of my greatest friends in prison. Several were MK men who had been arrested in 1964. These included Mac Maharaj (below right), a member of the SACP and one of the sharpest minds in the struggle.

We were handed picks and shovels and given rudimentary instructions. The lime itself, which is the soft, calcified residue of seashells and coral, is buried in layers of rock, and one had to break through to it with a pick, and then extract the seam of lime with a shovel. This was far more strenuous than the work in the courtyard, and after our first few days on the quarry we fell asleep immediately after our supper at 4.30 in the afternoon. We woke the next morning aching and still tired.

The authorities never explained why we had been taken from the courtyard to the quarry. They may simply have needed extra lime for the island's roads. We assumed it was another way of enforcing discipline, of showing us that we were no different from the general prisoners, who worked in the island's stone quarry. It was an attempt to crush our spirits.

But those first few weeks at the quarry had the opposite effect on us. Despite blistered and bleeding hands, we were invigorated. I much preferred being outside, being able to see grass and trees, to observe birds flitting overhead, to feel the wind blowing in from the sea.

Within a few days we were walking to the quarry, rather than going by truck, and this too was a tonic. During our twenty-minute march we got a better sense of the island, and could see the dense brush and tall trees that covered our home, and smell the eucalyptus blossoms, spot the occasional springbok or kudu grazing in the distance. Although some of the men regarded the march as drudgery, I never did.

Shortly after we started working at the quarry, we were joined by a number of other prominent political prisoners. Several were MK men who had been arrested in July 1964 and convicted of more than fifty acts of sabotage in what became known as the 'little Rivonia Trial'. These included Mac Maharaj, a member of the SACP and one of the sharpest minds in the struggle; Laloo Chiba, also a member of the MK high command and a stalwart colleague who proved a great asset in prison; and Wilton Mkwayi. We were also joined by Eddie Daniels, a Coloured member of the Liberal Party, who had been convicted for sabotage operations undertaken by the African Resistance Movement, a small sabotage group composed of members of the Liberal Party. Eddie was to become one of my greatest friends in prison.

After we had been sent to Robben Island, there was concern among our supporters that we would not be permitted to study. Within a few months of our arrival, the authorities announced that those who wanted to study could apply for permission. Most of the men did so, and even though they were D group prisoners, permission was granted. The state thought giving us study privileges would be harmless. Later, they came to regret it. Within months, virtually all of us were studying for one qualification or another. At night, our cell block seemed more like a study hall than a prison.

But the privilege of studying came with a host of conditions. Certain subjects, such as politics or military history, were prohibited. For years, we were not permitted to receive funds except from our families, so that poor prisoners rarely had money for books or tuition. Nor were we permitted to lend books to other prisoners, which would have enabled our poorer colleagues to study.

Prisoners were permitted to enrol at either the University of South Africa (UNISA) or the Rapid Results College, which was for those studying for their high school qualification. In my own case, studying under the auspices of the University of London was a mixed blessing. On the one hand I was assigned the sorts of stimulating books that would not have been on a South African reading list; on the other, the authorities inevitably regarded many of them as unsuitable and thus banned them.

In addition to books, we were permitted to order publications necessary to our studies. The authorities were extremely strict about this. But one day Mac Maharaj told a comrade who was studying economics to request the *Economist*. We laughed and said we might as well ask for *Time* magazine, because the *Economist* was also a newsweekly. But Mac simply smiled and said the authorities wouldn't know that; they judged a book by its title. Within a month, we were receiving the *Economist* and reading the news we hungered for. But the authorities soon discovered their mistake and ended the subscription.

We regarded it as our duty to keep in touch with our men in groups F and G, where the general prisoners were kept, but communication between sections was a serious violation of regulations. We formed a clandestine communications committee, composed of Kathy, Mac Maharaj, Laloo Chiba and several others, and their job was to organize all such practices.

One of the first techniques was engineered by Kathy and Mac, who began secretly collecting empty matchboxes. Mac had the idea of constructing a false bottom to the box and placing in it a tiny written message. Laloo Chiba wrote minuscule coded messages that would be placed in the converted matchbox. Joe Gqabi, another MK soldier who was with us, would carry the matchboxes on our walks to the quarry and drop them at a strategic crossing where we knew the general prisoners would pass. Designated prisoners from F and G would pick up the matchboxes on their walks, and we retrieved messages in the same fashion. It was far from perfect, and we could easily be foiled by something as simple as the rain. We soon evolved more efficient methods.

We looked for moments when the warders were inattentive. One such time was during and after meals. We worked out a scheme whereby comrades from the general section who worked in the kitchen began placing letters and notes wrapped in plastic at the bottom of the food drums. We sent return communications in a similar way, wrapping notes in the same plastic and placing them at the bottom of the mounds of dirty dishes.

Our toilets and showers were adjacent to the isolation section. Prisoners from the general section were often sentenced to isolation there and would use the same set of toilets we did. Mac devised a method of wrapping notes in plastic and then taping them

Communication between the sections was a serious violation of regulations. We found many effective ways round the ban. One technique was to write in tiny coded script on toilet paper. The paper was so small and easily hidden that this became a popular way of smuggling out messages.

inside the rim of the toilet bowl. We encouraged our political comrades in the general section to be charged and placed in isolation so that they could retrieve these notes and send replies.

Another technique was to write in tiny coded script on toilet paper. The paper was so small and easily hidden that this became a popular way of smuggling out messages. When the authorities discovered a number of these communications, they took the extraordinary measure of rationing toilet paper.

But even with all these ingenious methods, one of the best ways was getting sent to the prison hospital. The island had one hospital, and it was difficult to segregate us from the general prisoners while we were there. Sometimes prisoners from the different sections even shared the same wards, and men from section B and prisoners from F and G mingled and exchanged information about political organizations, strikes, go-slows, whatever the current prison issues were.

In July 1966 I had my second visit from my wife. It was almost exactly two years after the first, and it nearly did not happen at all. Winnie had been under constant harassment since her first visit in 1964. Her sisters and brother were persecuted by the police, and the authorities attempted to forbid anyone in her family from living with her. Some of the nastiest items were known to me because when I returned from the quarry, I would often find neatly cut clippings about Winnie on my bed.

This second visit was for only half an hour, and we had much to discuss. Winnie was a bit agitated from the rough treatment in Cape Town and the fact that, as always, she had to travel in the hold of the ferry where the fumes from the engine made her ill. She had taken pains to dress up for me, but she looked thin and drawn.

We reviewed the education of the children, the health of my mother, which was not very good, and our finances. A critical issue was the education of Zeni and Zindzi. Winnie had placed the girls in a school designated as Indian, and the authorities were harassing the principal on the grounds that it was a violation of the law for the school to accept 'African' pupils. We made the difficult decision to send Zeni and Zindzi to boarding school in Swaziland. This was hard on Winnie, who found her greatest support in the two girls.

As always, when the warder yelled 'Time up!', I thought only a few minutes had passed. I always preferred Winnie to leave first so that she would not have to see me led away, and I watched as she whispered a good-bye, hiding her pain from the warders.

Soon after the visit, I learned that Winnie had been charged for failing to report to the police on her arrival in Cape Town as well as refusing to furnish the police with her address when she left.

Winnie was arrested and released on bail. She was tried and sentenced to a year's imprisonment, which was suspended except for four days. Winnie was subsequently dismissed from her second job as a social worker because of the incident, and lost her main source of income.

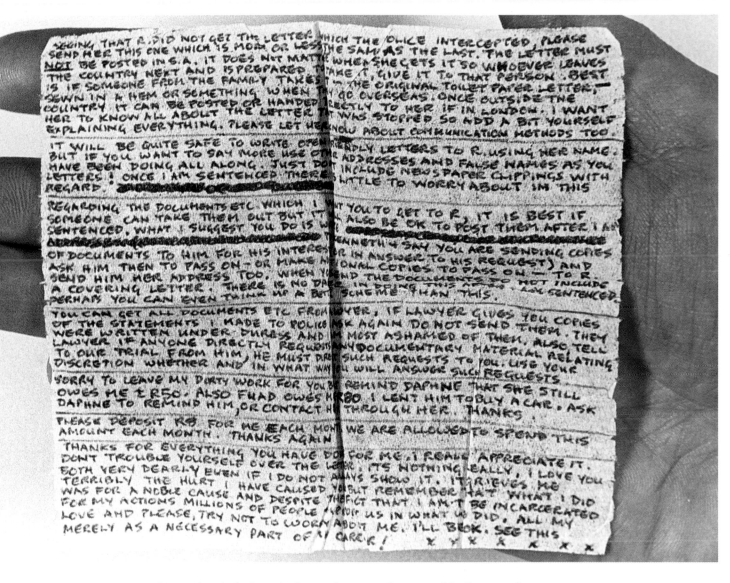

By 1966, the warders had adopted a laissez-faire attitude: we could talk as much as we wanted as long as we worked. We would cluster in small groups, four or five men in a rough circle, and talk all day long, about every subject under the sun. We were constantly engaged in political debates. I have always enjoyed the cut-and-thrust of debating, and was a ready participant.

One of our earliest and longest debates concerned the relationship between the ANC and the Communist Party. Some of the men, especially those MK soldiers who had been trained in socialist countries, believed that the ANC and the party were one and the same. Even some very senior ANC colleagues, such as Govan Mbeki and Harry Gwala, subscribed to this theory.

The party did not exist as a separate entity on Robben Island. In prison, there was no point in making the distinction between the ANC and the party that existed on the outside. My own views on the subject had not altered in many years. The ANC was a mass liberation movement that welcomed all those with the same objectives.

Over time, the debate concerning the ANC and the party grew progressively

acrimonious. A number of us proposed one way to resolve it: we would write to the ANC in exile in Lusaka. We prepared a secret twenty-two-page document on the subject with a covering letter from myself to be sent to Lusaka. It was a risky manoeuvre to prepare and smuggle out such a document. In the end, Lusaka confirmed the separation of the ANC and the party and the argument died.

Another recurrent political discussion was whether or not the ANC leadership should come exclusively from the working class. Some argued that because the ANC was a mass organization made up mainly of ordinary workers, the leadership should come from those same ranks. My argument was that it was as undemocratic to specify that the leaders had to be from the working class as to declare that they should be bourgeois intellectuals. If the movement had insisted on such a rule, most of its leaders, men such as Chief Luthuli, Moses Kotane, Dr Dadoo, would have been ineligible. Revolutionaries are drawn from every class.

That spring, we had felt a certain thawing on the part of the authorities, a relaxation of the iron-fisted discipline that had prevailed on the island. The tension between prisoners and warders had lessened somewhat. But this lull proved to be short-lived and it came to an abrupt end one morning in September. We had just put down our picks and shovels and were walking to the shed for lunch. As one of the general prisoners wheeled a drum of food towards us, he whispered, 'Verwoerd is dead.' We looked at each other in disbelief and glanced over at the warders, who seemed unaware that anything momentous had occurred.

Later, we heard about the obscure white parliamentary messenger who stabbed Verwoerd to death, and we wondered at his motives. Although Verwoerd thought Africans were lower than animals, his death did not yield us any pleasure. Political assassination is not something I or the ANC have ever supported.

As often happened on the island, we had learned significant political news before our own guards. But by the following day it was obvious the warders knew, for they took out their anger on us. The tension that had taken months to abate was suddenly at full force. The authorities began a crackdown against political prisoners as though we had held the knife that stabbed Verwoerd.

The authorities always imagined that we were secretly linked with all kinds of powerful forces on the outside. The spate of successful guerrilla attacks against the South African police forces in Namibia by the South West African People's Organization (SWAPO) - an ally of the ANC - had also unnerved them.

The punishment against us was never spelled out as an official policy, but it was a renewal of the harsh atmosphere that had prevailed upon our arrival on the island. A vicious martinet called van Rensburg was flown to the island at twenty-four hours' notice after the assassination. His reputation preceded him, for his name was a byword among prisoners for brutality. Van Rensburg was a big, clumsy, brutish fellow who did not speak but shouted. During his first day on the job we noticed he had a small swastika tattooed on his wrist. But he did not need this offensive symbol to prove his cruelty. His job was to

make our lives as wretched as possible, and he pursued that goal with great enthusiasm.

Van Rensburg was vindictive in large ways and small. When our lunch arrived at the quarry and we would sit down to eat - we now had a simple wooden table - van Rensburg would inevitably choose that moment to urinate next to our food.

One of the few ways prisoners can take their revenge on warders is through humour, and van Rensburg became the butt of many of our jokes. Among ourselves we called him 'Suitcase'. Warders' lunch boxes were known as 'suitcases' and normally a warder would designate a prisoner to carry his 'suitcase'. But we always refused to carry van Rensburg's 'suitcase', hence the nickname.

One morning in early 1967 we were preparing to walk to the quarry when Suitcase informed us that an order had come down from Major Kellerman forbidding us to talk.

The cemetery for lepers and other former inhabitants of the island (above). In the 19th century the island was used to house lepers and mental patients.

Not only was conversation banned on our walks; henceforth, there would be no conversation permitted at the quarry. 'From now on, silence!' he yelled.

This command was greeted by profound dismay and outrage. Talking and discussing issues were the only things that made the work at the quarry tolerable. During our lunch break Major Kellerman himself appeared and walked into our lunch shed. With a cough of embarrassment, he announced that his order had been a mistake and that we could resume talking at the quarry, just as long as we did it quietly. We were glad the order was rescinded, but suspicious as to why.

That afternoon, I discovered that my cell had been moved from No. 4, near the entrance of the passage, to No. 18, at the back. As always, there was no explanation. We guessed that we were to have a visitor and I had been moved because the authorities did not want me to be the first among the prisoners to talk to whoever was coming. If each prisoner in turn voiced his complaints, the authorities could yell 'Time up!' before a visitor reached cell No. 18. We resolved that in the interest of unity, each individual along the passage would inform any visitor that while everyone had individual complaints, the prisoner in No. 18 would speak for all.

The main gate of the prison (above).

The following morning after breakfast, we were informed by Suitcase that we would not be going to the quarry. Then Major Kellerman appeared to say that Mrs Helen Suzman, the only member of the liberal Progressive Party in Parliament and the lone parliamentary voice of true opposition to the Nationalists, would be arriving shortly. In less than fifteen minutes, Mrs Suzman came through the door of our corridor, accompanied by General Steyn, the commissioner of prisons. As she was introduced to each prisoner, she asked him whether he had any complaints. Each man replied in the same way: 'I have many complaints, but our spokesman is Mr Nelson Mandela at the end of the corridor.' To General Steyn's dismay, Mrs Suzman was soon at my cell. She firmly shook my hand and cordially introduced herself.

Unlike judges and magistrates, who were automatically permitted access to prisons, members of Parliament had to request permission to visit a prison. Mrs Suzman was one of the few, if not the only, member of Parliament who took an interest in the plight of political prisoners. Many stories were circulating about Robben Island, and Mrs Suzman had come to investigate for herself.

This was Mrs Suzman's first visit to Robben Island, but she was utterly unfazed by her surroundings, and proposed that we get down to business right away. General Steyn and the commanding officer stood by her, but I did not mince words. I told her of our desire to have the food improved and equalized and to have better clothing, the need for facilities for studying, our lack of rights to information such as newspapers and many more things.

I told her of the harshness of the warders, and mentioned van Rensburg in particular. Normally I would not complain about an individual warder, but van Rensburg was in a class by himself.

Mrs Suzman listened attentively, jotting down what I said in a small notebook, and promised to take these matters up with the minister of justice. She then made an inspection of our cells, and talked a bit with some of the other men. It was a wonderful sight to see this courageous woman peering into our cells and strolling around our courtyard. She was the first and only woman ever to grace our cells.

We later learned that Mrs Suzman had taken up our case in Parliament, and within a few weeks of her visit, Suitcase was transferred off the island.

I never imagined the struggle would be either short or easy. The first few years on the island were difficult times both for the organization outside and those of us in prison. After Rivonia, much of the movement's underground machinery had been destroyed. Our structures had been discovered and uprooted; those who were not captured were scrambling to stay one step ahead of the enemy. Virtually every one of the ANC's senior leaders was either in jail or in exile.

The old church. Stern and God-fearing, the Afrikaner takes his religion seriously. Every Sunday morning a minister from a different denomination would preach to us. During the first two years on the island we were not allowed to leave our cells for Sunday services. The minister would preach from the head of the corridor. By the third year, services were held in the courtyard.

In the years after Rivonia, the ANC's External Mission, formerly responsible for fund-raising, diplomacy and establishing a military training programme, took up the reins of the organization as a whole. The External Mission not only had to create an organization in exile, but had the even more formidable task of trying to revitalize the underground ANC inside South Africa.

The state had grown stronger. The police had become more powerful, their methods more ruthless, their techniques more sophisticated. The South African Defence Force was expanding. The economy was stable, the white electorate untroubled. The South African government had powerful allies in Great Britain and the United States who were content to maintain the status quo.

But elsewhere the struggle against imperialism was on the march. In the middle to late 1960s armed struggles were being fought throughout southern Africa. In Namibia (then South West Africa), SWAPO was making its first incursions into the Caprivi Strip; in Mozambique and Angola the guerrilla movement was growing and spreading. In Zimbabwe (then Rhodesia), the battle against white minority rule was advancing. Ian Smith's white government was bolstered by the South African Defence Force, and the ANC regarded the battle in Zimbabwe as an extension of our struggle at home. In 1967 we learned that the ANC had forged an alliance with the Zimbabwe African People's Union (ZAPU), which had been formed by Joshua Nkomo.

That year, a group of MK soldiers who had been training in Tanzania and Zambia crossed the Zambezi River into Rhodesia with the intention of making their way home. This first group of MK soldiers was christened the Luthuli Detachment and they were the spearhead of the armed struggle. In August, as the Luthuli Detachment, accompanied by ZAPU troops, moved southward, they were spotted by the Rhodesian army. Over the next few weeks, fierce battles were fought and both sides sustained casualties. Finally, our troops were overpowered by the superior numbers of the Rhodesian forces. Some were captured, and others retreated into Bechuanaland – which had become independent Botswana. By the beginning of 1968 another, larger, ANC detachment had entered Rhodesia and fought not only the Rhodesian army but South African policemen who had been posted to Rhodesia.

We heard of this months later by rumour, but did not learn the full story until some of the men who had fought there were imprisoned with us. Though our forces were not victorious, we quietly celebrated the fact that our MK cadres had engaged the enemy in combat on their own terms. It was a milestone in the struggle. 'Justice' Panza, one of the commanders of the Luthuli Detachment, was later imprisoned with us. He briefed us on the detachment's military training, political education and valour in the field. As a former commander-in-chief of MK, I was terribly proud of our soldiers.

Before receiving the news of MK's battles abroad, we also learned of Chief Luthuli's death at home in July 1967. I was granted permission to write a letter to his widow. Luthuli's death left a great vacuum in the organization. Yet in Oliver Tambo, who was acting president-general of the ANC, the organization found a man who could fill the chief's shoes. Like Luthuli, he was articulate yet not showy, confident but humble. He too epitomized Chief Luthuli's precept: 'Let your courage rise with danger.'

The ANC formed its own internal organization on Robben Island. Known as the High Command or, more officially, the High Organ, it consisted of the most senior ANC leaders on the island, the men who had been members of the National Executive: Walter Sisulu, Govan Mbeki, Raymond Mhlaba and me. I served as the head of the High Organ.

From its inception, we decided the High Organ would not try to influence external ANC policy. We had no reliable way of evaluating the situation in the country, and concluded it would be neither fair nor wise for us to offer guidance on matters about which we were uninformed. Instead, we made decisions about such matters as prisoners' complaints, strikes, mail, food – all the day-to-day concerns of prison life. We would, when possible, convene a general members' meeting, which we regarded as vital to the health of our organization. But as these meetings were extremely dangerous and thus infrequent, the High Organ would often take decisions that were then communicated to all the other members. The High Organ also operated a cell system, with each cell consisting of three members.

Time may seem to stand still for those of us in prison, but it did not halt for those outside. I was reminded of this when I was visited by my mother in spring 1968. I had not seen her since the end of the Rivonia Trial, and when one doesn't see one's family for many years at a time, the transformation can be striking. My mother suddenly seemed very old.

She had journeyed all the way from the Transkei, accompanied by my son Makgatho, my daughter Makaziwe and my sister Mabel. Because I had four visitors and they had come a great distance, the authorities extended the visiting time from half an hour to forty-five

❝ One cold morning in July 1969, I was called to the main office on Robben Island and handed a telegram. It was from my youngest son, Makgatho. He informed me that my first and oldest son, Madiba Thembekile, whom we called Thembi, had been killed in a motor accident in the Transkei. Thembi was then twenty-five, and the father of two small children. What can one say about such a tragedy? I was already overwrought about my wife, I was still grieving for my mother, and then to hear such news. I do not have words to express the sorrow, or the loss I felt. It left a hole in my heart that can never be filled. I returned to my cell and lay on my bed. I do not know how long I stayed there, but I did not emerge for dinner. Some of the men looked in, but I said nothing. Finally, Walter came to me and knelt beside my bed, and I handed him the telegram. He said nothing, but only held my hand. I do not know how long he remained with me. There is nothing that one man can say to another at such a time. ❞

minutes. I had not seen my son and daughter since before the trial and they had become adults in the interim, growing up without me.

My mother had lost a great deal of weight, which concerned me. Her face appeared haggard. Only my sister Mabel seemed unchanged. While it was a great pleasure to see all of them and to discuss family issues, I was uneasy about my mother's health.

I spoke to Makgatho and Maki about my desire for them both to pursue further schooling and asked Mabel about relatives in the Transkei. The time passed far too quickly. As with most visits, the greatest pleasure often lies in the recollection of it, but this time, I could not stop worrying about my mother. I feared that it would be the last time I would ever see her.

Several weeks later, after returning from the quarry, I was told to go to head office to collect a telegram. It was from Makgatho, informing me that my mother had died of a heart attack. I immediately made a request to the commanding officer to be permitted to attend her funeral in the Transkei, which he turned down.

A mother's death causes a man to look back on and evaluate his own life. Her difficulties, her poverty, made me question once again whether I had taken the right path. That was always the conundrum: had I made the right choice in putting the people's welfare even before that of my own family? For a long time, my mother had not understood my commitment to the struggle. My family had not asked for or even wanted to be involved in the struggle, but my involvement penalized them.

But I came back to the same answer. In South Africa it is hard for a man to ignore the needs of the people, even at the expense of his own family. I had made my choice and, in the end, she had supported it. But that did not lessen the sadness I felt at not being able to make her life more comfortable, or the pain of not being able to lay her to rest.

In the early hours of the morning of 12 May 1969 the security police woke Winnie at our home in Orlando and detained her without charge under the 1967 Terrorism Act, which gave the government unprecedented powers of arrest and detention without trial. The raid, I later learned, was part of a nationwide crackdown in which dozens of others were detained, including Winnie's sister. She was placed in solitary confinement in Pretoria, where she was denied bail and visitors; over the next weeks and months she was relentlessly and brutally interrogated.

When Winnie was finally charged – six months later – I managed to send instructions for her to be represented by Joel Carlson, a long-time anti-apartheid lawyer. Winnie and twenty-two others were charged under the Suppression of Communism Act for attempting to revive the ANC. Later, George Bizos and Arthur Chaskalson, both members of the Rivonia team, joined the defence. In October, seventeen months after her arrest, the state withdrew its case without explanation, and Winnie was released. Within two weeks, she was again banned, and placed under house arrest. She immediately applied for permission to visit me but was rebuffed.

There was nothing I found so agonizing in prison as the thought that Winnie was in prison too. I put a brave face on the situation, but inwardly I was deeply disturbed and worried. Nothing tested my inner equilibrium as much as the time that Winnie was in solitary confinement. Although I often urged others not to worry about what they could not control, I was unable to take my own advice. I had many sleepless nights. What were the authorities doing to my wife? How would she bear up? Who was looking after our daughters? Who would pay the bills?

Brigadier Aucamp allowed me to send letters to Winnie, and relayed one or two from her. Normally, prisoners awaiting trial are not permitted mail, but Aucamp permitted it as a favour to me. I was grateful, but knew the authorities had not granted permission out of altruism: they were reading our letters, hoping to glean some information that would assist their case against Winnie.

During this time I experienced another grievous loss. One July day I received a telegram from my youngest son Makgatho to say that Thembi, my eldest son, had been killed in a car accident. He was twenty-five. I asked permission to attend my son's funeral, but permission was denied. All I could do was write to Thembi's mother, Evelyn, and tell her that I shared her suffering.

Robben Island: Beginning to Hope

There in front of us, glinting in the morning light, we saw the ocean, the rocky shore, and in the distance, winking in the sunshine, the glass towers of Cape Town (opposite). Although it was surely an illusion, the city, with Table Mountain looming behind it, looked agonizingly close, as though one could almost reach out and grasp it.

The graph of improvement in prison was never steady. Progress was halting, and typically accompanied by setbacks. But conditions did improve. We had won a host of small battles that added up to a change in the atmosphere of the island. While we did not run it, the authorities could not run it without us, and in the aftermath of van Rensburg's departure, our life became more tolerable.

One morning, instead of walking to the quarry, we were ordered into the back of a truck. It rumbled off in a new direction, and fifteen minutes later we were ordered to jump out. There in front of us, glinting in the morning light, we saw the ocean, the rocky shore, and in the distance, the glass towers of Cape Town.

We had been brought to the shore to collect seaweed. After fishing out the seaweed from the shallows, we lined it up in rows on the beach. When it was dry, we loaded it into the back of the truck. It was then shipped to Japan, where it was used as a fertilizer.

The work could be quite strenuous, but that hardly mattered because we had the pleasures and distractions of a panoramic tableau: ships trawling, oil tankers moving slowly across the horizon; gulls spearing fish from the sea and seals cavorting on the waves. We marvelled at the daily drama of the weather over Table Mountain, with its shifting canopy of clouds and sun.

In the summer the water felt wonderful, but in winter the icy Benguela Current made wading out into the waves a torture. The rocks were jagged, and we often cut and scraped our legs as we worked. But we preferred the sea to the quarry, although we never spent more than a few days there at a time.

I had not seen Zindzi (above left with Winnie and Zenani) since she was three years old. I put on a fresh shirt that morning and took more trouble than usual with my appearance: I did not want to look like an old man for my youngest daughter.

The ocean proved to be a treasure chest. I found beautiful pieces of coral and elaborate shells, which I sometimes brought back to my cell. Once someone discovered a bottle of wine stuck in the sand. Jeff Masemola of the PAC was an extremely talented artist and sculptor and the authorities allowed him to harvest pieces of driftwood, which he carved into fantastic figures, some of which the warders offered to buy.

The atmosphere at the shore was more relaxed than at the quarry. We also relished the seaside because we ate extremely well there. Each morning when we went to the shore, we would take a large drum of fresh water. Later we would bring along a second drum, which we would use to make a kind of Robben Island seafood stew. For our stew we would pick up clams, mussels and abalone. We also caught crayfish, which hid in the crevices of rocks.

We would take our catch and pile it into the second drum. Wilton Mkwayi, the chef among us, would concoct the stew. When it was ready, the warders would join us and we would all sit down on the beach and have a kind of picnic lunch.

In the struggle, Robben Island was known as 'the University'. This was not only because of what we learned from books, or because prisoners studied English, Afrikaans, art, geography and mathematics, or because so many of our men like Billy Nair, Ahmed Kathrada, Mike Dingake and Eddie Daniels earned multiple degrees. Robben Island was known as 'the University' because of what we learned from each other. We became our own faculty, with our own professors, our own curriculum, our own courses. We made a distinction between academic studies, which were official, and political studies, which were not.

Our university grew up partly out of necessity. As young men came to the island, we realized that they knew very little about the history of the ANC. Walter, perhaps the greatest living historian of the ANC, began to tell them about the genesis of the organization and its early days. Gradually this informal history grew into a course of study, which became known as Syllabus A, involving two years of lectures on the ANC and the liberation struggle. Syllabus A also included a course taught by Kathy, 'A History of the Indian Struggle'. Another comrade added a history of the Coloured people. Mac, who had studied in the German Democratic Republic, taught a course on Marxism.

Teaching conditions were not ideal. Study groups would work together at the quarry and station themselves in a circle around the leader of the seminar.

In addition to my informal studies, my legal work continued. I sometimes considered hanging a name-plate outside my cell, because I was spending so many hours a week preparing judicial appeals for other prisoners, though this was forbidden under prison service regulations.

The oppression of my wife did not let up. In 1974 Winnie was charged with violating her banning orders, which restricted her from having any visitors apart from her children and

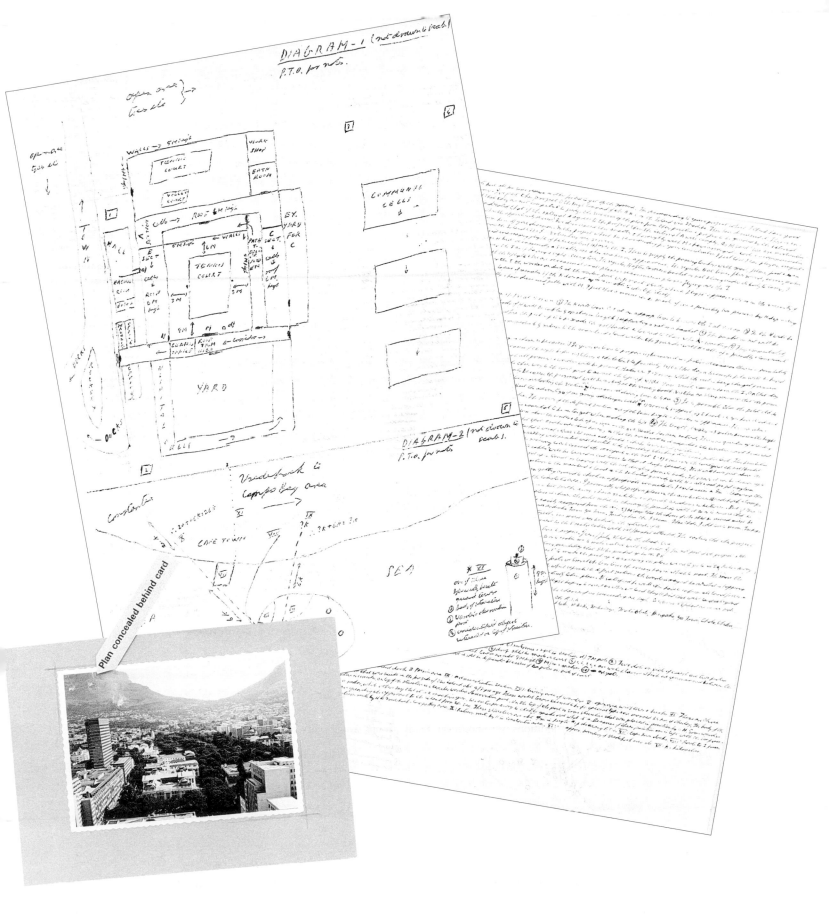

Plan concealed behind card

her doctor. She was then working at a lawyer's office, and a friend brought Zeni and Zindzi to see her during her lunch hour. For this, Winnie was sentenced to six months' imprisonment. She was put in Kroonstad Prison in the Orange Free State, but her experience there was not as horrendous as her previous stay in Pretoria.

When Winnie was released in 1975, we managed, through letters and communications with our lawyers, to work out a plan for me to see Zindzi. I had not seen Zindzi since she was three years old. Prison regulations stated that no child between the ages of two and sixteen might visit a prisoner. When I went to Robben Island, all my children were in this legal limbo of age restrictions.

In 1975, Zindzi turned fifteen. Birth records are not kept in a very organized way for Africans, and Winnie found that it was not hard to modify her documents to show that Zindzi was born a year earlier. She applied for a permit, and it was approved.

I had not seen Winnie for over a year, and I was pleased to find that she looked well. But I was delighted to behold what a beautiful woman my youngest daughter had become. I knew she would be feeling uncomfortable, and I did my best to lighten the atmosphere. I asked her questions about her life, her schooling and her friends, and then tried to take her back to the old days that she hardly remembered. I told her how I often recalled Sunday mornings at home when I dandled her on my knee. I recollected small incidents and adventures in Orlando when she was a baby, and how she had rarely cried even when she was small. Through the glass, I could see her holding back her tears as I talked.

In 1975, when I turned fifty-seven, Walter and Kathy approached me with a long-term plan that would make my sixtieth birthday memorable.

One of the issues that always concerned us was how to keep the idea of the struggle before the people. During the previous decade, the government had silenced most of the radical press, and there remained a proscription on publishing the words or pictures of any banned or imprisoned individuals. An editor could go to jail and his newspaper be closed down for publishing so much as a snapshot of me or my colleagues.

Walter and Kathy suggested that I ought to write my memoirs, and said that the perfect time for such a book to be published would be on my sixtieth birthday. Walter said that such a story would serve to remind people of what we had fought and were still fighting for. He added that it could become a source of inspiration for young freedom fighters. The idea appealed to me, and I agreed to go ahead.

When I decide to do something, I like to start immediately, and I threw myself into this new project. I decided to write most of the night and sleep during the day. During the first week or two I would take a nap after dinner, wake at 10 p.m. and then write until it was time for breakfast. After working at the quarry, I would then sleep until dinner, and the process would begin again. After a few weeks of this, I notified the authorities that I was not feeling well and would not be going to the quarry. They did not seem to care, and from then on I was able to sleep most of the day.

❛ Birthday celebrations were bare-bone affairs on Robben Island. In lieu of cake and gifts, we would pool our food and present an extra slice of bread or cup of coffee to the birthday honouree. Fikile Bam and I were born on the same date, 18 July, and I would save a few sweets that I had purchased at Christmas for the two of us to share on our common anniversary. ❜

We created an assembly line to process the manuscript. Each day I passed what I wrote to Kathy, who reviewed it and then read it to Walter. Kathy then wrote their comments in the margins. Walter and Kathy have never hesitated to criticize me, and I took their suggestions to heart, often incorporating their changes. This marked-up manuscript was then given to Laloo Chiba, who spent the next night transferring my writing to his own almost microscopic shorthand, reducing ten pages of foolscap to a single small piece of paper. It would be Mac's job to smuggle the manuscript to the outside world.

The warders grew suspicious. They asked Mac, 'What is Mandela up to? Why is he sitting up late at night?' But Mac said he had no idea. I wrote rapidly, completing a draft in four months, covering the period from my birth through to the Rivonia Trial, and ending with some notes about Robben Island.

Mac hid the transcribed version of the manuscript inside the binding of a number of notebooks he used for his studies. In this way, he was able to conceal the entire text from the authorities and smuggle it out when he was released in 1976. The arrangement was that Mac would secretly communicate when the manuscript was safely out of the country; only then would we destroy the original. In the meantime, we still had to dispose of a five-hundred-page manuscript. We did the only thing we thought we could do: we buried it in the garden in the courtyard. Surveillance in the courtyard had become careless. The warders usually sat talking in an office at the northern end, from which they could not see the southern end, where there was a small garden. It was there that I decided to bury the manuscript.

We decided to bury the manuscript in three separate places. We divided it into segments, each wrapped in plastic, and placed them inside empty cocoa containers. One morning after breakfast, Kathy, Walter, Eddie Daniels and I drifted over to the garden at the southern end of the courtyard where we appeared to be having a political discussion. We were hiding the manuscript in our shirts. At a signal from me, we bent down and began digging. I dug in the centre, near a manhole cover that led to a drainpipe. When I reached the pipe, I carved out a space beneath it, and it was there that I placed the largest of the three containers. The others dug two shallower holes for their portions.

We finished just in time to line up for our march to the quarry. As I walked that morning, I felt a sense of relief that the manuscript was safely hidden. I then thought no more about it.

A few weeks later, I heard a sound in the courtyard that made me uneasy: it was the thud of picks and shovels. There, at the south end of the courtyard, was a work crew from the general section. To my alarm, they were digging in the area where the manuscript was buried.

The authorities had decided to build a wall in front of the isolation section because they had discovered that the prisoners in isolation were able to communicate with us in the courtyard. The work crew was digging a shallow trench for the concrete foundation of the wall.

> ❝ I relived my experiences as I wrote about them. Those nights, as I wrote in silence, I could once again experience the sights and sounds of my youth in Qunu and Mqhekezweni; the excitement and fear of coming to Johannesburg; the tempests of the Youth League; the endless delays of the Treason Trial; the drama of Rivonia. It was like a waking dream and I attempted to transfer it to paper as simply and truthfully as I could. ❞

While washing, I managed to inform Walter and Kathy about the digging outside. Kathy thought that the main part of the manuscript, which was buried under the pipe, would probably be safe, but that the other two were vulnerable. When the drums of breakfast porridge were wheeled into the courtyard, the warders in charge of the work crew ordered the men out of the yard to prevent any fraternization with the political prisoners.

With our bowls of porridge in hand, I led Walter and Kathy over to the south end of the courtyard as though I wanted to confer with them privately. The beginnings of the trench were already perilously close to the two smaller containers. There was only one thing to do: as inconspicuously as possible, the four of us began digging. We managed to unearth the two containers fairly quickly, and covered the area again with soil. To rescue the manuscript under the pipe would require more time, but we were confident that they would not find it because they would not have to dislodge the pipe in order to build the wall.

We hid the manuscript in our shirts as we walked back to our cells. Eddie was not going to the quarry that day, and we gave the containers to him, instructing him to destroy them as soon as possible. I breathed more easily knowing that we had salvaged the two containers, and tried not to dwell on the remaining piece of manuscript as I worked that day.

When we returned from the quarry that afternoon, I strolled over to the far end of the courtyard. I attempted to appear as casual as possible, but I was alarmed by what I saw. The prisoners had dug a trench that ran parallel to the wall of the isolation section and had actually removed the pipe altogether. They could not help but uncover the manuscript.

Early the next morning, I was summoned to the office to see the commanding officer. Next to him stood a high prison official who had just arrived from Pretoria. The commanding officer announced: 'Mandela, we have found your manuscript.' He then reached behind his desk and produced a sheaf of papers.

'This is your handwriting, is it not?' he demanded. Again, I remained silent. 'Mandela,' the commander said in some exasperation. 'We know this is your work.'

'Well,' I replied, 'you must produce some proof of that.'

They scoffed at this, and said they knew the notations in the margin had been made by Walter Sisulu and Ahmed Kathrada.

Although he did not impose a penalty that day, a short while later Walter, Kathy and I were called before General Rue, the deputy commissioner of prisons, who told us that we had abused our study privileges in order to write the manuscript illegally. For that offence, our study privileges were being suspended indefinitely. As it turned out, we lost study privileges for four years.

After Mac was released in December, he sent the notebooks overseas to England. He spent the next six months under house arrest in South Africa before slipping out of the country and going first to Lusaka to see Oliver Tambo, and then to London. He stayed there for six months; with a typist, he reconstructed the manuscript and put together a

On 16 June 1976 fifteen thousand schoolchildren gathered in Soweto to protest at the government's ruling that half of all classes in secondary schools must be taught in Afrikaans. Students did not want to learn and teachers did not want to teach in the language of the oppressor. Pleadings and petitions by parents and teachers had fallen on deaf ears. A detachment of police confronted this army of earnest schoolchildren and without warning opened fire, killing thirteen-year-old Hector Pieterson (right) and many others. The children fought with sticks and stones, and mass chaos ensued, with hundreds of children wounded and killed and two white men stoned to death.

typescript. He then returned to Lusaka and presented Oliver with a copy. From there, the trail grows cold. I heard nothing from Lusaka about the manuscript and still don't know precisely what Oliver did with it. Although it was not published while I was in prison, it forms the basis of this memoir.

In June 1976 we began to hear vague reports of a great uprising in the country. It was only when the first young prisoners who had been involved in the 16 June uprising began to arrive on Robben Island in August that we learned what had truly happened.

The events of that day reverberated in every town and township of South Africa. The uprising triggered riots and violence across the country. Mass funerals for the victims of state violence became national rallying points. Suddenly the young people of South Africa were fired with the spirit of protest and rebellion. Students boycotted schools all across the country. ANC organizers joined with students to actively support the protest. Bantu Education had come back to haunt its creators, for these angry and audacious young people were its progeny.

In September, the isolation section was filled with young men who had been arrested in the aftermath of the uprising. Through whispered conversations we learned first-hand what had taken place. My comrades and I were enormously cheered; the spirit of mass protest that had seemed dormant during the 1960s was erupting in the 1970s. Many of these young people had left the country to join our own military movement, and then smuggled themselves back. Thousands of them were trained in our camps in Tanzania, Angola and Mozambique. There is nothing so encouraging in prison as learning that the people outside are supporting the cause for which you are inside.

These young men were a different breed of prisoner from those we had seen before. They were brave, hostile and aggressive; they would not take orders, and shouted 'Amandla!' at every opportunity. Their instinct was to confront rather than cooperate. The authorities did not know how to handle them, and they turned the island upside down.

The new prisoners were appalled by what they considered the barbaric conditions of the island, and said they could not understand how we could live in such a way. We told them that they should have seen the island in 1964. But they were almost as sceptical of us as they were of the authorities. It was obvious that they regarded us as moderates. After so many years of being branded a radical revolutionary, this was a novel and not altogether pleasant feeling.

When some of these men, such as Strini Moodley of the South African Students' Organization and Saths Cooper of the Black People's Convention, came into our section, I asked them to give us papers on their movement and philosophy. I wanted to know what had brought them to the struggle, what motivated them, what their ideas were for the future.

Shortly after their arrival on the island, the commanding officer came to me and asked me as a favour to address the young men. He wanted me to tell them to restrain themselves, to recognize the fact that they were in prison and to accept the discipline of prison life. I told him that I was not prepared to do that. Under the circumstances, they would have regarded me as a collaborator of the oppressor.

This was our first exposure to the Black Consciousness Movement. With the banning of the ANC, PAC and Communist Party, the Black Consciousness Movement helped fill a vacuum among young people. Black Consciousness was less a movement than a philosophy and grew out of the idea that blacks must first liberate themselves from the sense of psychological inferiority bred by three centuries of white rule. Only then could the people rise in confidence and truly liberate themselves from repression. While the Black Consciousness Movement advocated a non-racial society, they excluded whites from playing a role in achieving that society.

These concepts were not unfamiliar to me: they closely mirrored ideas I myself had held at the time of the founding of the ANC Youth League a quarter of a century before.

But just as we had outgrown our Youth League outlook, I was confident that these young men would transcend some of the strictures of Black Consciousness. While I was encouraged by their militancy, I thought that their philosophy, in its concentration on blackness, was sectarian, and represented an intermediate view that was not fully mature. I saw my role as an elder statesman who might help them move on to the more inclusive ideas of the Congress Movement. I knew also that these young men would eventually become frustrated because Black Consciousness offered no programme of action, no outlet for their protest.

Some of the men who arrived were already well known in the struggle. I had heard reports of the bravery of Patrick 'Terror' Lekota, a leader of the South African Students' Organization, and sent him a note of welcome to Robben Island.

Terror's nickname came from his prowess on the soccer field, but he was just as formidable in a debate. He disagreed with some of his colleagues on the issue of racial exclusiveness and inched closer to the ideas of the ANC. Once on the island, Terror decided that he wanted to join us, but we discouraged him – not because we did not want him but because we thought such a manoeuvre would create tensions in the general section.

But Terror would not take no for an answer and publicly switched his allegiance to the ANC. One day, not long afterwards, he was assaulted with a garden fork by disgruntled BCM members. The authorities charged the attackers and planned to put them on trial, but in the interest of harmony, we advised Terror not to lodge a complaint. He agreed, and refused to testify against those who had hurt him. The case was dropped. Such a trial, I felt, would only play into the hands of the authorities.

After that incident, the floodgates seemed to open and dozens of BCM men decided to join the ANC, including some of those who had planned the attack on Terror. Terror rose to the top of the ANC hierarchy in the general section, and was soon teaching ANC policies to other prisoners. The courage and vision of men like him confirmed to us that our views remained potent, and still represented the best hope for unifying the liberation struggle as a whole.

In their anxiousness to deal with these young lions, the authorities more or less let us fend for ourselves. We were in the second year of a go-slow strike at the quarry, demanding a complete end to all manual labour. Our requirement was for the right to do something useful with our days, such as studying or learning a trade. We no longer even went through the motions of working at the quarry; we simply talked among ourselves. In early 1977, the authorities announced the end of manual labour. Instead, we could spend our days in our section. They arranged some type of work for us to do in the courtyard, but it was merely a figleaf to hide their capitulation.

The end of manual labour was liberating. I could now spend the day reading, writing letters, discussing issues with my comrades or formulating legal briefs. The free time allowed me to pursue what became two of my favourite hobbies on Robben Island: gardening and tennis.

Almost from the beginning of my sentence on Robben Island, I asked the authorities for permission to start a garden in the courtyard. For years, they refused, but eventually they relented, and we were able to cut out a small garden on a narrow patch of earth against the far wall.

A garden was one of the few things in prison that one could control. To plant a seed, watch it grow, to tend it and then harvest it offered a simple but enduring satisfaction. The sense of being the custodian of this small patch of earth offered a small taste of freedom.

In some ways, I saw the garden as a metaphor for certain aspects of my life. A leader must also tend his garden; he, too, sows seeds, and then watches, cultivates and harvests the result. Like the gardener, a leader must take responsibility for what he cultivates; he must mind his work, try to repel enemies, preserve what can be preserved and eliminate what cannot succeed.

I wrote Winnie two letters about a particularly beautiful tomato plant, how I coaxed it from a tender seedling to a robust plant that produced deep red fruit. But, then, either through some mistake or lack of care, the plant began to wither and decline, and nothing I did would bring it back to health. When it finally died, I removed the roots from the soil, washed them and buried them in a corner of the garden.

I narrated this small story at great length. I do not know what she read into that letter, but when I wrote it I had a mixture of feelings: I did not want our relationship to go the way of that plant, and yet I felt that I had been unable to nourish many of the most important relationships in my life. Sometimes there is nothing one can do to save something that must die.

At roughly the same time as we stopped working at the quarry, one of the warders had the idea of converting our courtyard (above) into a tennis court. Prisoners from the general section painted the cement green and then fashioned the traditional configuration of white lines. I had played a bit of tennis when I was at Fort Hare, but I was by no means an expert. But I pursued the sport for exercise, not style; it was the best and only replacement for the walks to and from the quarry.

In the wake of the Soweto student uprising, I learned that Winnie, along with my old friend and physician, Dr Nthato Motlana, had become involved with the Black Parents' Association, an organization of concerned local professionals and church leaders who acted as a guiding hand and intermediary for the students. The authorities seemed to be equally wary of the parents association and the young rebels. In August, less than two months after the student revolt, Winnie was detained under the Internal Security Act and imprisoned without charge in the Fort in Johannesburg, where she was held for five months. During that time I was able to write to her and my daughters, who were at boarding school in Swaziland, expressing support and solidarity. I was greatly distressed by her imprisonment, though she was apparently not mistreated this time and emerged from jail in December even firmer in her commitment to the struggle.

Though banned, Winnie picked up where she left off, and the authorities were dismayed about her popularity with the young radicals of Soweto. They were determined to lessen her influence and did it with a brazen and shameless act: they sent her into internal exile. She was being banished to a remote township in the Free State called Brandfort.

Brandfort is about two hundred and fifty miles southwest of Johannesburg, just north of Bloemfontein, in the Free State. After a long and rough ride, Winnie, Zindzi and all their possessions were dumped in front of a three-room tin-roofed shack in Brandfort's bleak African township, a desperately poor and backward place where the people were under the

On the night of 16 May 1977 police cars and a truck pulled up outside the house in Orlando West and began loading furniture and clothing into the back of the truck. This time Winnie was not being arrested, detained or interrogated. She was being banished. In Brandfort she and Zindzi would be alone.

Winnie's three-room
tin-roofed shack in
Brandfort's African
township.

thumb of the local white farmers. Winnie was regarded with wariness and trepidation. The local language was Sesotho, which Winnie did not speak.

Her new circumstances saddened and angered me. At least when she was home in Soweto, I could picture her cooking in the kitchen or reading in the lounge; I could imagine her waking up in the house I knew so well. That was a source of comfort to me. In Soweto, even if she was banned, there were friends and family near by. In Brandfort she and Zindzi would be alone.

In 1978 Zeni, my second-youngest daughter and my first child with Winnie, married Prince Thumbumuzi, a son of King Sobhuza of Swaziland. They had met while Zeni was away at school.

There was a tremendous advantage in Zeni becoming a member of the Swazi royal family: she was immediately granted diplomatic privileges and could visit me virtually at will. That winter, after she and Thumbumuzi were married, they came to see me, along with their newborn baby daughter. We were allowed to meet one another in the consulting room, not the normal visiting area. I waited for them with some nervousness.

It was a truly wondrous moment when they came into the room. I stood up, and when Zeni saw me, she practically tossed her tiny daughter to her husband and ran across the room to embrace me. I had not held my daughter since she was about her own daughter's age. It was a dizzying experience.

The visit had a more official purpose and that was for me to choose a name for the child. It is the custom for the grandfather to select a name, and the one I had chosen was Zaziwe – which means 'Hope'. The name had a special meaning for me, for during all my years in prison hope never left me – and now it never would. I was convinced that this child would be a part of a new generation of South Africans for whom apartheid would be a distant memory – that was my dream.

In 1978 we learned via the intercom that P. W. Botha (below right) had succeeded John Vorster (below left) as prime minister.

In 1978, after we had spent almost fifteen years agitating for the right to receive news, the authorities offered us a compromise. Instead of permitting us to receive newspapers or listen to radio, they started their own radio news service, which consisted of a daily canned summary of the news read over the prison's intercom system.

The broadcasts were far from objective or comprehensive. Several of the island's censors would compile a brief news digest from other daily radio bulletins. The broadcasts consisted of good news for the government and bad news for all its opponents.

That year, we learned that P. W. Botha had succeeded John Vorster as prime minister. What the warders did not tell us was that Vorster resigned as a result of press revelations about the Department of Information's misuse of government funds. I knew little about Botha apart from

the fact that he had been an aggressive defence minister and had supported a military strike into Angola in 1975. We had no sense that he would be a reformer in any way.

But even without our expurgated radio broadcasts, we had learned what the authorities did not want us to know. We learned of the successful liberation struggles in Mozambique and Angola in 1975 and their emergence as independent states with revolutionary governments. The tide was turning our way.

In 1980 we were granted the right to buy newspapers. This was a victory but, as always, each new privilege contained within it a catch. The new regulation stated that A group prisoners were granted the right to buy one English-language newspaper and one Afrikaans newspaper a day. But the annoying caveat was that any A group prisoner found sharing his newspaper with a non-A group prisoner would lose his newspaper privileges. We protested against this restriction, but to no avail.

We received two daily newspapers: *Cape Times* and *Die Burger*. Both were conservative papers, especially the latter. Yet the prison censors went through each of those newspapers every day with scissors, clipping out articles that they deemed unsafe for us to see. By the time we received them, they were filled with holes. We were soon able to supplement these papers with copies of the *Star*, the *Rand Daily Mail* and the *Sunday Times*, but these papers were even more heavily censored.

One story I was certainly not able to read was in the *Johannesburg Sunday Post* in March 1980. The headline was 'FREE MANDELA!' Inside was a petition that people could sign to ask for my release and that of my fellow political prisoners. While newspapers were still barred from printing my picture or any words I had ever said or written, the *Post*'s campaign ignited a public discussion of our release.

The idea had been conceived in Lusaka by Oliver Tambo and the ANC, and the campaign was the cornerstone of a new strategy that would put our cause in the forefront of people's minds. The ANC had decided to personalize the quest for our release by centring the campaign on a single figure. There is no doubt that the millions of people who subsequently became supporters of this campaign had no idea of precisely who Nelson Mandela was.

The previous year I had been awarded the Jawaharlal Nehru Human Rights Award in India, another piece of evidence of the resurgence of the struggle. I was of course refused permission to attend the ceremony, as was Winnie, but Oliver accepted the award in my absence. We had a sense of a reviving ANC.

The campaign for our release rekindled our hopes. During the harsh days of the early 1970s, when the ANC seemed to sink into the shadows, we had to force ourselves not to give in to despair. In many ways we had miscalculated; we had thought that by the 1970s we would be living in a democratic, non-racial South Africa. Yet as we entered the new decade my hopes for that South Africa rose once again. Some mornings I walked out into the courtyard and every living thing there, the seagulls and wagtails, the small trees, and even the stray blades of grass seemed to smile and shine in the sun. It was at such times, when I perceived the beauty of even this small, closed-in corner of the world, that I knew that some day my people and I would be free.

In March 1982, I was told by the prison authorities that my wife had been in a car accident, and that she was in hospital. They had very little information, and I had no idea of her condition or what her circumstances were. I accused the authorities of holding back information, and made an urgent application for my attorney to visit me. The authorities used information as a weapon, and it was a successful one. I was preoccupied with my wife's health until I was visited on 31 March by Winnie's attorney and my friend Dullah Omar.

Dullah quickly eased my mind about Winnie. She had been in a car that had overturned, but she was all right.

The Johannesburg Sunday Post in March 1980. I am told that when 'Free Mandela' posters went up in London, most people thought my Christian name was 'Free'.

Our visit was brief, and as I was led back to section B my mind was still dwelling on Winnie, and I was plagued by the feeling of powerlessness and my inability to help her.

I had not been in my cell long when I was visited by the commanding officer and a number of other prison officials. This was highly unusual; the CO did not generally pay calls on prisoners in their cells. I stood up when they arrived, and the commander actually entered my cell. There was barely room for the two of us.

'Mandela,' he said, 'I want you to pack up your things.'

I asked him why.

'We are transferring you,' he said simply.

'Where?'

'I cannot say,' he replied.

I demanded to know why. He told me only that he had received instructions from Pretoria that I was to be transferred off the island immediately. The commanding officer left and went in turn to the cells of Walter, Raymond Mhlaba and Andrew Mlangeni and gave them the same order.

I was disturbed and unsettled. What did it mean? Where were we going? In prison, one can only question and resist an order to a certain point, then one must succumb. We had no warning, no preparation. I had been on the island for over eighteen years, and to leave so abruptly?

We were each given several large cardboard boxes in which to pack our things. Everything that I had accumulated in nearly two decades could fit into these few boxes. We packed in little more than half an hour.

There was a commotion in the corridor when the other men learned we were leaving, but we had no time to say a proper good-bye to our comrades of many years. This is another one of the indignities of prison. The bonds of friendship and loyalty with other prisoners count for nothing with the authorities.

Within minutes we were on board the ferry headed for Cape Town. I looked back at the island as the light was fading, not knowing whether I would ever see it again. A man can get used to anything, and I had grown used to Robben Island. I had lived there for almost two decades and while it was never a home – my home was in Johannesburg – it had become a place where I felt comfortable. I have always found change difficult, and leaving Robben Island, however grim it had been at times, was no exception. I had no idea what to look forward to.

At the docks, surrounded by armed guards, we were hustled into a windowless truck. The four of us stood in the dark while the truck drove for what seemed considerably more than an hour. We passed through various checkpoints, and finally came to a stop. The back doors swung open, and in the dark we were marched up some concrete steps and through metal doors into another security facility. I managed to ask a guard where we were.

'Pollsmoor Prison', he said.

Talking with the Enemy

Political violence and international pressure continued to intensify. Members of the Leandra Youth Congress (below) at the funeral of their community leader, Chief Mayise, in Leandra township, Transvaal, 25 January 1986.

Pollsmoor maximum security prison is on the edge of a prosperous white suburb called Tokai, a few miles southeast of Cape Town. The four of us had been given a spacious room on the third and topmost floor. We were the only prisoners on the entire floor. The room was clean and modern, about fifty by thirty feet and had a separate section with a toilet, urinal, two basins and two showers. There were four beds, with sheets, and towels, a great luxury for men who had spent much of the last eighteen years sleeping on thin mats on a stone floor. Compared with Robben Island, we were in a five-star hotel.

We also had our own terrace, as long as half a soccer field, where we were allowed out during the day. It had white concrete walls about twelve feet high, so that we could see only the sky, except in one corner where we could make out the ridges of the Constantiaberge mountains.

Though we were now on the mainland, we felt more isolated. We spent those early weeks speculating on why we had been transferred. We knew the authorities had long resented and feared the influence we had on younger prisoners. But the reason seemed to be more strategic: we believed the authorities were attempting to cut off the head of the ANC on the island by removing its leadership. Robben Island itself was becoming a sustaining myth in the struggle, and they wanted to rob it of some of its symbolic import. Walter, Raymond and I were members of the High Organ, but the one piece that did not fit was the presence of Mlangeni. Andrew was not a member of the High Organ and had not been in the forefront of the island leadership.

A few months later we were joined by Kathy, who had indeed been a member of the High Organ. We were also joined by a man who had not even come from Robben Island. Patrick Maqubela was a young lawyer and ANC member from the eastern Cape. Maqubela was serving a twenty-year sentence for treason and had been transferred to Pollsmoor from Diepkloof in Johannesburg, where he had made waves by organizing prisoners. Patrick was a bright, amiable, undaunted fellow with whom we got along very well. It could not have been easy for him bunking in with a group of old men who had been together for two decades.

We were now in a world of concrete. I missed the natural splendour of Robben Island. But our new home had many consolations. For one thing, the food at Pollsmoor was far superior; after years of eating pap three meals a day, Pollsmoor's dinners of proper meat and vegetables were like a feast. We were permitted a fairly wide range of newspapers and magazines, and could receive such previously contraband publications as *Time* magazine and the *Guardian Weekly* from London. This gave us a window on the wider world. We also had a radio, but one that received only local stations and not what we really wanted: the BBC World Service. There was not even a pretence that we had to work. I had a small cell that functioned as a study, with a chair, desk and bookshelves, where I could read and write during the day.

I was visited by Winnie shortly after arriving at Pollsmoor and was pleased to find that the visiting area was far better and more modern than the one on Robben Island. We had a large glass barrier and far more sophisticated microphones so that we did not have to strain to hear. It was far easier for my wife and family to get to Pollsmoor than to Robben Island, and this made a tremendous difference. The supervision of visits also became more humane.

Within a few weeks of surveying all the empty space we had on the roof and how it was bathed in sun the whole day, I decided to start a garden and received permission to do so from the commanding officer. I requested that the prison service supply me with sixteen forty-four-gallon oil drums that they sliced in half for me. The authorities then filled each half with rich, moist soil, creating in effect thirty-two giant flowerpots. I grew onions, aubergines, cabbage, cauliflower, beans, spinach, carrots, cucumbers, broccoli, beetroot, lettuce, tomatoes, peppers, strawberries, and much more.

Each morning, I put on a straw hat and rough gloves and worked in the garden for two hours. Every Sunday I would supply vegetables to the kitchen so that they could cook a special meal for the common-law prisoners. I also gave quite a lot of my harvest to the warders, who used to bring satchels to take away their fresh vegetables.

In May 1984, I found some consolation that seemed to make up for all the discomforts. On a scheduled visit from Winnie, Zeni and her youngest daughter, I was escorted into a separate room where there was only a small table, and no dividers of any kind. That day was the beginning of what were known as 'contact' visits. Winnie actually got a fright,

> **'** Pollsmoor maximum security prison is set amid the strikingly beautiful scenery of the Cape, between the mountains of Constantiaberge to the north and hundreds of acres of vineyards to the south a few miles from C. T. But this natural beauty was invisible to us behind Pollsmoor's high concrete walls. At Pollsmoor I first understood the truth of Oscar Wilde's haunting line about the tent of blue that prisoners call the sky. **'**

thinking that I was perhaps ill. But before either of us knew it, we were in the same room and in each other's arms. I kissed and held my wife for the first time in all these many years. It was a moment I had dreamed about a thousand times. I held her to me for what seemed like an eternity. We were still and silent except for the sound of our hearts. I did not want to let go of her at all, but I broke free and embraced my daughter and then took her child onto my lap. It had been twenty-one years since I had even touched my wife's hand.

At Pollsmoor, we were more connected to outside events. We were aware that the struggle was intensifying, and that the efforts of the enemy were similarly increasing. In 1981, the South African Defence Force launched a raid on ANC offices in Maputo, Mozambique, killing thirteen of our people, including women and children. In December 1982, MK set off explosions at the unfinished Koeberg nuclear power plant outside Cape Town and placed bombs at many other military and apartheid targets around the country. That same month, the South African military again attacked an ANC outpost in Maseru, Lesotho, killing forty two people, including a dozen women and children.

Funeral of a member of alleged ANC guerillas, killed in a shoot-out with the police.

In August 1982 the activist Ruth First was opening her post in Maputo, where she was living in exile, when she was murdered by a letter bomb. Ruth, the wife of Joe Slovo, was a brave anti-apartheid activist who had spent a number of months in prison.

MK's first car bomb attack took place in May 1983, and was aimed at an air force and military intelligence office in the heart of Pretoria. This was an effort to retaliate for the unprovoked attacks the military had launched on the ANC in Maseru and elsewhere and was a clear escalation of the armed struggle. Nineteen people were killed and more than two hundred injured.

The killing of civilians was a tragic accident, and I felt a profound horror at the death toll. But disturbed as I was by these casualties, I knew that such accidents were the inevitable consequence of the decision to embark on a military struggle.

Both the government and the ANC were working on two tracks: military and political. On the political front, the government was pursuing its standard divide-and-rule strategy in attempting to separate Africans from Coloureds and Indians. In a referendum in November 1983, the white electorate endorsed P. W. Botha's plan to create a so-called tricameral Parliament, with Indian and Coloured chambers in addition to the white Parliament. This was an effort to lure Indians and Coloureds into the system, and divide them from Africans. But the offer was merely a 'toy telephone', as all parliamentary action by Indians and Coloureds was subject to a white veto. It was also a way of fooling the outside world into thinking that the government was reforming apartheid. Botha's ruse did not deceive the people, as more than 80 per cent of eligible Indian and Coloured voters boycotted the election to the new houses of Parliament in 1984.

Powerful grassroots political movements were being formed inside the country that had firm links to the ANC, the principal one being the United Democratic Front, of which I was named a patron. The UDF had been created to coordinate protest against the new apartheid constitution in 1983, and the first elections to the segregated tricameral Parliament in 1984. The UDF soon blossomed into a powerful organization that united over six hundred anti-apartheid organizations – trade unions, community groups, church groups, student associations.

The ANC was experiencing a new birth of popularity. Opinion polls showed that the Congress was far and away the most popular political organization among Africans even though it had been banned for a quarter of a century. The anti-apartheid struggle as a whole had captured the attention of the world; in 1984 Bishop Desmond Tutu was awarded the Nobel Peace Prize. The South African government was under growing international pressure, as nations all across the globe began to impose economic sanctions on Pretoria.

UDF poster. The UDF had been created to coordinate protest against the new apartheid constitution in 1983. It soon blossomed into a powerful organization.

The government had sent 'feelers' to me over the years, beginning with Minister Kruger's efforts to persuade me to move to the Transkei. These were not efforts to negotiate, but attempts to isolate me from my organization. Although I did not respond to these overtures, the mere fact that they were talking rather than attacking could be seen as a prelude to genuine negotiations.

In late 1984 and early 1985 I had visits from two prominent Western statesmen, Lord Nicholas Bethell, a member of the British House of Lords and the European Parliament, and Samuel Dash, a professor of law at Georgetown University and a former counsel to the US Senate Watergate Committee. Both visits were authorized by the new minister of justice, Kobie Coetsee, who appeared to be a new sort of Afrikaner leader.

Faced with trouble at home and pressure from abroad, P. W. Botha offered a tepid, halfway measure. On 31 January 1985, in a debate in Parliament, the state president publicly offered me my freedom if I 'unconditionally rejected violence as a political instrument'. This offer was extended to all political prisoners.

I wrote to the foreign minister, Pik Botha, rejecting the conditions for my release, while also preparing a public response. Botha's offer was an attempt to drive a wedge between me and my colleagues by tempting me to accept a policy the ANC rejected. I wanted to reassure the ANC in general and Oliver Tambo in particular that my loyalty to

the organization was beyond question. I also wished to send a message to the government that while I rejected its offer because of the conditions attached to it, I nevertheless thought negotiation, not war, was the path to a solution.

I intended to make it clear that if I emerged from prison into the same circumstances under which I was arrested, I would be forced to resume the same activities for which I was arrested.

I met Winnie and Ismail Ayobi, my lawyer, on a Friday; on Sunday, a UDF rally was to be held in Soweto's Jabulani Stadium, where my response would be made public. I gave Ismail and Winnie the speech I had prepared. On Sunday 10 February 1985, my daughter Zindzi read my response to a cheering crowd of people who had not been able to hear my words legally anywhere in South Africa for more than twenty years. Zindzi was a dynamic speaker like her mother, and said that her father should be at the stadium to speak the words himself.

In 1985 after a routine medical examination from the prison doctor, I was referred to a urologist, who diagnosed an enlarged prostate gland and recommended surgery. He said the procedure was routine.

Police beat up a woman in the townships, which were in upheaval with protest.

On 31 January 1985
P. W. Botha publicly
offered me my freedom if
I 'unconditionally rejected
violence as a political
instrument'. I wrote to the
foreign minister, Pik Botha,
rejecting the conditions
for my release, while
also preparing a public
response. Botha's offer
was an attempt to drive
a wedge between me
and my colleagues.
On Sunday 10 February
1985 my daughter Zindzi
read my speech at the
UDF rally in Soweto.

I was taken to Volks Hospital in Cape Town under heavy security. Winnie flew down and was able to see me prior to the surgery. But I had another visitor, a surprising one: Kobie Coetsee, the minister of justice. Not long before, I had written to Coetsee pressing him for a meeting to discuss talks between the ANC and the government. That morning, he dropped by the hospital as if he were visiting an old friend. Though I acted as though this was the most normal thing in the world, I was amazed. The government, in its slow and tentative way, was reckoning that they had to come to some accommodation with the ANC.

Although we did not discuss politics, I did bring up one sensitive issue, and that was the status of my wife. In August, shortly before I entered hospital, Winnie had gone to Johannesburg to receive medical treatment. The only trips she was permitted from Brandfort were to visit either me or her doctor. While in Johannesburg, her house in Brandfort and the clinic behind it were firebombed and destroyed. Winnie had nowhere to live, and she decided to remain in Johannesburg despite the fact that the city was off-limits to her. Nothing happened for a few weeks, and then the security police wrote to inform her that the house in Brandfort had been repaired and she must return. But she refused to do so. I asked Coetsee to allow Winnie to remain in Johannesburg. He said he could promise nothing, but he would look into it.

I spent several days in hospital recuperating. When I was discharged, I was collected from the hospital by Brigadier Munro. Commanding officers do not usually pick up prisoners from hospitals, so my suspicions were immediately aroused. Upon my return to Pollsmoor I was taken to a new cell away from my friends on the ground floor of the prison, three floors below and in an entirely different wing. Why had the state taken this step?

It would be too strong to call it a revelation, but over the next few weeks I decided that the change was not a liability but an opportunity. I was not happy to be separated from my colleagues, and I missed my garden and the sunny terrace. But my solitude gave me a certain liberty, and I resolved to use it to do something I had been pondering for a long while: begin discussions with the government. If we did not start a dialogue soon, both sides would be plunged into a dark night of oppression, violence and war. My solitude would give me an opportunity to take the first steps in that direction, without the scrutiny that might destroy such efforts.

A decision to talk to the government was of such importance that it should only have been made in Lusaka. But I had neither the time nor the means to communicate fully with Oliver.

I was now in a kind of splendid isolation. In order to see my colleagues, three floors above, I had to put in a formal request for a meeting, which had to be approved by head office in Pretoria. Walter, Kathy and Ray were angry that we had been separated. They wanted to lodge a strong protest, and demand that we be reunited. My response was not what they expected. 'Look, chaps,' I said, 'I don't think we should oppose this thing. Perhaps something good will come of this. I'm now in a position where the government can make an approach to us.'

I chose to tell no one what I was about to do. Not my colleagues upstairs nor those in Lusaka. The ANC is a collective, but the government had made collectivity impossible. I did not have the security or the time to discuss these issues with my organization. I knew that my colleagues upstairs would condemn my proposal, and that would kill my initiative even before it was born. There are times when a leader must move out ahead of the flock, go off in a new direction, confident that he is leading his people the right way. Finally, my isolation furnished my organization with an excuse in case matters went awry: the old man was alone and completely cut off, and his actions were taken by him as an individual, not a representative of the ANC.

Within a few weeks of my move, I wrote to Kobie Coetsee to propose talks about talks. As before, I received no response. I wrote once more, and again there was no response. I realized I had to look for another opportunity to be heard. That came in early 1986.

At a meeting of the British Commonwealth in Nassau in October 1985, the leaders could not reach agreement on whether to participate in international sanctions against South Africa. This was mainly because Margaret Thatcher was adamantly opposed. To resolve the deadlock, the assembled nations agreed that a delegation of 'eminent persons' would visit South Africa and report back on whether sanctions were the appropriate tool to help bring about the end of apartheid. In early 1986 the seven-member Eminent Persons Group, led by General Olusegun Obasanjo, the former military leader of Nigeria, and the former Australian Prime Minister Malcolm Fraser, arrived in South Africa on their fact-finding mission.

In February, I was visited by General Obasanjo to discuss the nature of the delegation's brief. He was eager to facilitate a meeting between me and the full group. With the government's permission, such a meeting was scheduled for May. The group would be talking with the cabinet after they had seen me, and I viewed this as a chance to raise the subject of negotiations.

At the meeting between me and the Eminent Persons Group, we were joined briefly by two significant observers: Kobie Coetsee, and Lieutenant General W. H. Willemse, the commissioner of prisons. Before they took their leave, I told them the time had come for negotiations, not fighting, and that the government and the ANC should sit down and talk.

The Eminent Persons Group had come with many questions involving the issues of violence, negotiations and international sanctions. At the outset, I set the ground rules for our discussions. 'I am not the head of the movement,' I told them. 'The head of the movement is Oliver Tambo in Lusaka. You must go and see him. You can tell him what my views are, but they are my personal views alone. They don't even represent the views of my colleagues here in prison. All that being said, I favour the ANC beginning discussions with the government.'

Various members of the group had concerns about my political ideology, and what a South Africa under ANC leadership might look like. I told them I was a South African nationalist, not a communist, that nationalists came in every hue and colour, and that I was

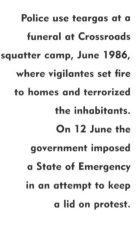

firmly committed to a non-racial society. I told them I believed in the Freedom Charter, which embodied principles of democracy and human rights, and that it was not a blueprint for socialism. I spoke of my concern that the white minority should feel a sense of security in any new South Africa. I told them I thought many of our problems were a result of lack of communication between the government and the ANC, and that some of these could be resolved through actual talks.

They questioned me extensively on the issue of violence, and while I was not yet willing to renounce violence, I affirmed in the strongest possible terms that violence could never be the ultimate solution to the situation in South Africa. While I once again reiterated that these were my views and not those of the ANC, I suggested that if the government withdrew the army and the police from the townships, the ANC might agree to a suspension of the armed struggle as a prelude to talks. I told them that my release alone would not stem the violence in the country or stimulate negotiations.

After the group had finished with me, they planned to see both Oliver in Lusaka and government officials in Pretoria. In my remarks, I had sent messages to both places. I wanted the government to see that under the right circumstances we would talk, and I wanted Oliver to know that my position and his were the same.

In May, the Eminent Persons Group was scheduled to see me one last time. I was optimistic, as they had been to both Lusaka and Pretoria, and I hoped that the seed of negotiations had been sown. But on the day the group was scheduled to meet cabinet ministers, the South African Defence Force, under the orders of President Botha, launched air raid and commando attacks on ANC bases in Botswana, Zambia and Zimbabwe. This utterly poisoned the talks, and the group immediately left South Africa. Once again, I felt my efforts to move negotiations forward had stalled.

Oliver Tambo and the ANC had called for the people of South Africa to render the country ungovernable, and the people were obliging. The state of unrest and political violence was reaching new heights. The anger of the masses was unrestrained; the townships were in upheaval. International pressure was growing stronger every day. On 12 June 1986 the government imposed a State of Emergency in an attempt to keep a lid on protest. The time seemed inauspicious for negotiations. But often, the most discouraging moments are precisely the time to launch an initiative. That month I wrote to General Willemse, the commissioner of prisons, saying merely, 'I wish to see you on a matter of national importance.'

That weekend, I was told by the commanding officer to be prepared to see General Willemse, who was coming down from Pretoria. Instead of conferring with the general in the visiting area, I was taken to his residence in the grounds of Pollsmoor itself. I told him I wanted to see Kobie Coetsee, the minister of justice, in order to raise the question of talks between the government and the ANC. The general telephoned the minister and the two spoke for a few moments. Minutes later, we left in his car, bound for the minister's house in Cape Town.

Coetsee greeted me warmly and we settled down on comfortable chairs in his lounge. I spent three hours in conversation with him and was struck by his sophistication and willingness to listen. He asked knowledgeable and relevant questions – questions that reflected a familiarity with the issues that divided the government and the ANC. He asked me under what circumstances we would suspend the armed struggle; whether or not I spoke for the ANC as a whole; whether I envisioned any constitutional guarantees for minorities in a new South Africa. His questions went to the heart of the issues dividing the government and the ANC.

Women from Crossroads camp protest outside the Parliament building, Cape Town, demanding protection from vigilantes and the right to rebuild their burnt-out homes.

I sensed that Coetsee wanted some resolution. 'What is the next step?' he asked. I told him I wanted to see the state president and the foreign minister, Pik Botha. Coetsee said he would send my request through the proper channels. I was greatly encouraged. In ghostly outline, I saw the beginnings of a compromise. But again, after this promising start, nothing happened. Weeks and then months passed without a word from Coetsee. In some frustration, I wrote him another letter.

Although I did not get a direct response from Kobie Coetsee, there were other signs. On the day before Christmas, Lieutenant Colonel Gawie Marx, the deputy commander of Pollsmoor, wandered by my cell after breakfast and said quite casually, 'Mandela, would you like to see the city?' I was not exactly certain what he had in mind, but I thought there was no harm in saying yes. I walked with the colonel through the fifteen locked metal doors between my cell and the entrance, and when we emerged, I found his car waiting for us.

We drove into Cape Town along the lovely road that runs parallel to the coast. He had no destination in mind and we simply meandered around the city in a leisurely fashion. It

The Reverend Marawu conducts an ANC funeral.

was absolutely riveting to watch the simple activities of people out in the world: old men sitting in the sun, women doing their shopping, people walking their dogs. I felt like a tourist in a strange and remarkable land.

As it turned out, that day in Cape Town was the first of many excursions. These trips were instructive. I saw how life had changed in the time I had been away, and because we mainly went to white areas, I saw the extraordinary wealth and ease that whites enjoyed. Though the country was in upheaval and the townships were on the brink of open warfare, white life went on placidly and undisturbed.

Much as I enjoyed these little adventures, I well knew that the authorities had a motive other than keeping me diverted. I sensed that they wanted to acclimatize me and perhaps get me so used to the pleasures of small freedoms that I might be willing to compromise in order to have complete freedom.

In 1987 I resumed contact with Kobie Coetsee. I had several private meetings with him at his residence, and later that year the government made its first concrete proposal. Coetsee said the government would like to appoint a committee of senior officials to conduct private discussions with me. This would be done with the full knowledge of the state president. He himself would be head of the committee, and it would include General

Willemse, the commissioner of prisons, Fanie van der Merwe, director general of the Prisons Department and Dr Niel Barnard, a former academic who was then head of the National Intelligence Service. The first three individuals were associated with the prison system, so if talks foundered or were leaked to the press, both sides would be able to cover up and say we were discussing prison conditions and nothing more.

The presence of Dr Barnard, however, disturbed me. He was the head of South Africa's equivalent of the CIA, and was also involved with military intelligence. I could justify discussions with the other officials, but not Barnard. His presence made the talks more problematic and suggested a larger agenda. I told Coetsee that I would like to think about the proposal overnight.

I considered all the ramifications. I knew that P. W. Botha had created something called the State Security Council, a shadowy secretariat of security experts and intelligence officials. He had done this, according to the press, to circumvent the authority of the cabinet and increase his own power. Dr Barnard was a key player in this inner council and was said to be a protégé of the president. I thought that my refusing Barnard would alienate Botha, and decided that such a tack was too risky. If the state president was not brought on board, nothing would happen. In the morning, I sent word to Coetsee that I accepted his offer.

Riot police confront workers leaving a May Day meeting in Johannesburg, May 1985. The Congress of South African Trade Unions (COSATU) had called for a work stoppage.

I knew that I had three crucial matters that I needed to address: first, I wanted to sound out my colleagues on the third floor before I proceeded any further, second, it was essential to communicate with Oliver in Lusaka about what was taking place and, finally, I intended to draft a memorandum to P. W. Botha laying out my views and those of the ANC on the vital issues before the country. This memorandum would create talking points for any future discussion.

I requested to see my colleagues, and I was allowed to see them one by one, not together. I would seek their counsel about the idea of having talks with the government without mentioning that an actual committee had been formed. Walter was first.

I have been through thick and thin with Walter. He was a man of reason and wisdom, and no man knew me better. There was no one whose opinion I trusted or valued more. I could see he was uncomfortable and, at best, lukewarm. 'In principle,' he said, 'I am not against negotiations. But I would have wished that the government initiated talks with us rather than our initiating talks with them.'

I replied that if he was not against negotiations in principle, what did it matter who initiated them? I told Walter that I thought we should move forward with negotiations and not worry about who knocked on the door first. Walter saw that my mind was made up and he said he would not stop me, but that he hoped I knew what I was doing.

Next was Raymond Mhlaba. 'Madiba,' he said, what have you been waiting for? We should have started this years ago.' Andrew Mlangeni's reaction was virtually the same as Ray's. The last man was Kathy. His response was negative; he was as resolutely against what I was suggesting as Raymond and Andrew were in favour.

Not long after this I received a note from Oliver Tambo that was smuggled to me by one of my lawyers. He had heard reports that I was having secret discussions with the government and he was concerned. He said he knew I had been alone for some time. Oliver's note was brief and to the point: what was I discussing with the government? The tenor of his note suggested that he thought I was making an error in judgment.

I replied to Oliver in a very terse letter saying that I was talking to the government about one thing and one thing only: a meeting between the National Executive of the ANC and the South African government.

The first formal meeting of the secret working group took place in May 1988, at Pollsmoor. While I knew both Coetsee and Willemse, I had never before met van der Merwe and Dr Barnard. The initial meeting was quite stiff, but in subsequent sessions we were able to talk more freely. I met them almost every week for a few months, and then at irregular intervals, sometimes not for a month, and then suddenly every week. The meetings were usually scheduled by the government, but sometimes I would request a session.

During our early meetings, I discovered that my new colleagues, with the exception of Dr Barnard, knew little about the ANC. They were all sophisticated Afrikaners, and far more open-minded than nearly all of their brethren. But they were the victims of so much propaganda that it was necessary to straighten them out about certain facts. Even Dr Barnard, who had made a study of the ANC, had received most of his information from police and intelligence files, which were in the main inaccurate and sullied by the prejudices of the men who had gathered them.

I was told in the winter of 1988 that P. W. Botha was planning to see me before the end of August. I was tense about seeing Mr Botha. He was known as 'die Groot Krokodil' – 'the Great Crocodile' – and I had heard many accounts of his ferocious temper. He seemed to me to be the very model of the old-fashioned, stiff-necked, stubborn Afrikaner who did not so much discuss matters with black leaders as dictate to them. His recent stroke had apparently only exacerbated this tendency. I resolved that if he acted in that finger-wagging fashion with me, I would have to inform him that I found such behaviour unacceptable.

I spent some time explaining our positions on the primary issues that divided the organization from the government. After these preliminaries, we focused on the critical issues: the armed struggle, the ANC's alliance with the Communist Party, the goal of majority rule and the idea of racial reconciliation.

The meetings had a positive effect: I was told in the winter of 1988 that President Botha was planning to see me before the end of August. The country was still in turmoil. The government had reimposed a State of Emergency in both 1987 and 1988. International pressure mounted. More companies left South Africa. The American Congress had passed a sweeping sanctions bill.

In 1987, the ANC celebrated its seventy-fifth anniversary and held a conference at the end of the year in Tanzania attended by delegates from more than fifty nations. Oliver declared that the armed struggle would intensify until the government was prepared to negotiate the abolition of apartheid.

I was suffering from a bad cough that I could not seem to shake off, and often felt too weak to exercise. I had complained about the dampness of my cell, but nothing had been done about it. One day, during a meeting with my attorney, Ismail Ayob, I felt ill and vomited.

I was taken to Tygerberg Hospital, on the campus of the University of Stellenbosch. The warders went in first and cleared everyone out of the entrance area. I was then escorted up to a floor that had been entirely emptied; the hall was lined with more than a dozen armed guards. It was discovered that I was in the very early stages of tuberculosis. The doctor agreed that it was probably the damp cell that had helped to cause my illness.

I spent the next six weeks at Tygerberg receiving treatment. In December, I was moved to the Constantiaberge Clinic, a luxurious facility near Pollsmoor that had never had a black patient before.

At Constantiaberge, I again began to meet Kobie Coetsee and the secret committee. While I was still at the clinic Coetsee said he wanted to put me in a situation that was halfway between confinement and freedom. I would not be so naive as to consider his proposal to be freedom, but I knew that it was a step in that direction.

In early December 1988, security on my ward was tightened and the officers on duty were more alert than usual. Some change was imminent. On the evening of 9 December, Major Marais came into my room and told me to prepare to leave. 'Where to?' I asked him. He could not say.

We left in a rush, and after about an hour on the road we entered a prison whose name I recognized: Victor Verster. Located in the lovely old Cape Dutch town of Paarl, Victor Verster is thirty-five miles northeast of Cape Town. The prison had the reputation of being a model facility. We drove through its entire length, and then along a winding dirt road through a rather wild, wooded area at the rear of the property. At the end of the road we came to an isolated whitewashed one-storey cottage set behind a concrete wall and shaded by tall fir trees.

> I was ushered into the house by Major Marais and found a spacious lounge next to a large kitchen, with an even larger bedroom at the back. The place was sparsely but comfortably furnished. It had not been cleaned or swept before my arrival, and the bedroom and living room were teeming with all kinds of exotic insects, centipedes, monkey spiders and the like. That night, I swept the insects off my bed and windowsill and slept extremely well in what was to be my new home. The next morning I surveyed my new abode and discovered a swimming pool in the back yard, and two smaller bedrooms. I walked outside and admired the trees that shaded the house and kept it cool. The entire place felt removed, isolated. The only thing spoiling the idyllic picture was that the walls were topped with razor wire, and there were guards at the entrance to the house. Even so, it was a lovely place and situation; a halfway house between prison and freedom.

That afternoon I was visited by Kobie Coetsee, who brought a case of Cape wine as a housewarming gift. The irony of a jailer bringing his prisoner such a gift was not lost on either of us. He told me that the cottage would be my last home before becoming a free man. The reason behind this move, he said, was that I should have a place where I could hold discussions in privacy and comfort.

The cottage did in fact give me the illusion of freedom. I could go to sleep and wake up as I pleased, swim whenever I wanted, eat when I was hungry – all were delicious sensations. Simply to be able to go outside during the day and take a walk when I desired was a moment of private glory. There were no bars on the windows, no jangling keys, no doors to lock or unlock. It was altogether pleasant, but I never forgot that it was a gilded cage.

The prison service provided me with a cook, Warrant Officer Swart, a tall, quiet Afrikaner who had once been a warder on Robben Island. He was a decent fellow without any prejudice and he became like a younger brother to me. He arrived at seven in the morning and left at four, and would make my breakfast, lunch and dinner. When I had

Sympathisers outside Tygerberg Hospital, where I spent six weeks receiving treatment for tuberculosis.

171

In 1989 the UDF formed an alliance with the Congress of South African Trade Unions (COSATU) to form the Mass Democratic Movement (MDM), which then began organizing a countrywide 'defiance campaign' of civil disobedience to challenge apartheid institutions.

visitors, which was increasingly often, he would prepare gourmet meals. When the authorities began to permit some of my ANC comrades and members of the United Democratic Front (UDF) and the Mass Democratic Movement (MDM) to visit, I accused them of coming only for the food.

The meetings with the committee continued, but we stalled on the same issues that had always prevented us from moving forward: the armed struggle, the Communist Party, and majority rule. I was still pressing Coetsee for a meeting with P. W. Botha. By this time, the authorities permitted me to have rudimentary communications with my comrades at Pollsmoor and Robben Island and also the ANC in Lusaka. Although I knew I was going ahead of my colleagues, I did not want to go too far, and find that I was all alone.

In January 1989, I was visited by my four comrades from Pollsmoor and we discussed the memorandum I was planning to send to the state president. It reiterated most of the points I had made in our secret committee meetings, but I wanted to make sure the state president heard them directly from me. He would see that we were not wild-eyed terrorists, but reasonable men.

'I am disturbed,' I wrote to Mr Botha in the memorandum 'as many other South Africans no doubt are, by the spectre of a South Africa split into two hostile camps – blacks on one side . . . and whites on the other, slaughtering one another.' To prepare the groundwork for negotiations, I proposed to deal with the three demands made of the ANC by the government as a precondition to negotiations: renouncing violence; breaking with the SACP; and abandoning the call for majority rule. I urged him to seize the opportunity without delay.

But delay there was. In January, P. W. Botha suffered a stroke. While it did not incapacitate the president, it did weaken him. In February Botha unexpectedly resigned as head of the National Party, but kept his position as state president. This was an unparalleled situation in the country's history. Some saw this as a positive development: that Botha wanted to be 'above party politics' in order to bring about true change in South Africa.

Political violence and international pressure both continued to intensify. Political detainees all across the country had held a successful hunger strike, persuading the minister of law and order to release over nine hundred detainees. In 1989 the UDF formed an alliance with the Congress of South African Trade Unions (COSATU) to form the Mass Democratic Movement (MDM), which then began organizing a countrywide 'defiance campaign' of civil disobedience to challenge apartheid institutions. On the international front, Oliver Tambo held talks with the governments of Great Britain and the Soviet Union, and in January 1987 met the US secretary of state, George Shultz, in Washington. The Americans recognized the ANC as an indispensable element of any solution in South Africa. Sanctions against South Africa remained in force and even increased.

On 4 July I was visited by General Willemse who informed me that I was being taken to see President Botha the following day. He described the visit as a 'courtesy call', and I was told to be ready to leave at 5.30 a.m. I thought I ought to have a suit and tie in which to see Mr Botha. The general agreed, and a short while later a tailor appeared to take my measurements. That afternoon I received a new suit, tie, shirt and shoes.

We drove from Victor Verster to Pollsmoor. After breakfast, in a small convoy, we drove to Tuynhuys, the official presidential office, and parked in an underground garage where we would not be seen. We took a lift to the ground floor and emerged in a grand wood-panelled lobby in front of the president's office. There we were met by Kobie Coetsee, Niel Barnard and a retinue of prison officials. I had spoken extensively with both Coetsee and Dr Barnard about this meeting, and they had advised me to avoid controversial issues. While we were waiting, Dr Barnard noticed that my shoelaces were not properly tied and he quickly knelt down to tie them for me. I realized just how nervous they were,

❝ That July, for my seventy-first birthday, I was visited at the cottage at Victor Verster by nearly my entire family. It was the first time I had ever had my wife and children and grandchildren all in one place, and it was a grand and happy occasion. Warrant Officer Swart outdid himself in preparing a feast, and he did not even get upset when I let some of the grandchildren eat their puddings before their main courses. After the meal, the grandchildren went into my bedroom to watch a video of a horror movie while the adults stayed outside gossiping in the lounge. It was a deep, deep pleasure to have my whole family around me, and the only pain was the knowledge that I had missed such occasions for so many years. ❞

and that did not make me any calmer. The door then opened and I walked in expecting the worst.

From the opposite side of his grand office, P. W. Botha walked towards me. He had planned his march perfectly, for we met exactly halfway. He had his hand out and was smiling broadly, and in fact, from that very first moment, he completely disarmed me.

We very quickly posed for a photograph of the two of us shaking hands. From the first, it was not as though we were engaged in tense political arguments but a lively and interesting tutorial. We did not discuss substantive issues so much as history and South African culture.

The meeting was not even half an hour long, and was friendly and breezy until the end. It was then that I raised a serious issue. I asked Mr Botha to release unconditionally all political prisoners; including myself. That was the only tense moment in the meeting, and Mr Botha said that he was afraid that he could not do that.

'Release Mandela' posters appeared everywhere.

While the meeting was not a breakthrough in terms of negotiations, it was one in another sense. Mr Botha had long talked about the need to cross the Rubicon, but he never did it himself until that morning at Tuynhuys. Now, I felt, there was no turning back.

A little more than a month later, in August 1989, P. W. Botha went on national television to announce his resignation as state president. The following day, F. W. de Klerk was sworn in as acting president and affirmed his commitment to change and reform.

Even as de Klerk became president, I continued to meet the secret negotiating committee. We were joined by Gerrit Viljoen, the minister of constitutional development, whose role was to bring our discussions into a constitutional framework. I pressed the government to display evidence of its good intentions by releasing my fellow political prisoners at Pollsmoor and Robben Island. I said the government could expect disciplined behaviour from them after their release.

On 10 October 1989, President de Klerk announced that Walter Sisulu and seven of my former Robben Island comrades, Raymond Mhlaba, Ahmed Kathrada, Andrew Mlangeni, Elias Motsoaledi, Jeff Masemola, Wilton Mkwayi and Oscar Mpetha, were to be released. That morning, I had been visited by Walter, Kathy, Ray and Andrew, and I was able to say good-bye. It was an emotional moment, but I knew I would not be too far behind. The men were released five days later from Johannesburg Prison. De Klerk had lived up to his promise, and the men were released under no bans; they could speak in the name of the ANC. It was clear that the ban on the organization had effectively expired, a vindication of our long struggle and our resolute adherence to principle.

The comrades are
finally released from
Robben Island,
October 1989.

In early December I was informed that a meeting with de Klerk was set for the twelfth of that month. By this time I was able to consult my colleagues, and had meetings at the cottage with my old colleagues and the leaders of the Mass Democratic Movement and the UDF. I received ANC people from all of the regions, as well as delegates from the UDF and COSATU.

I then drafted a letter to de Klerk not unlike the one I had sent to P. W. Botha. The subject was talks between the government and the ANC. I told the president that the current conflict was draining South Africa's lifeblood and that talks were the only solution. I said the ANC would accept no preconditions to talks, especially not the precondition that the government wanted: the suspension of the armed struggle. The government asked for an 'honest commitment to peace' and I pointed out that our readiness to negotiate was exactly that.

I reiterated my proposal that talks take place in two stages. I told him I fully supported the guidelines the ANC had adopted in the Harare Declaration of 1989, which put the onus on the government to eliminate the obstacles to negotiations that the state itself had created. Those demands included the release of all political prisoners, the lifting of all bans on restricted organizations and persons, the ending of the State of Emergency and the removal of all troops from the townships. I stressed that a mutually agreed-upon cease-fire to end hostilities ought to be the first order of business, for without that, no business could be conducted. The day before our meeting the letter was delivered to Mr de Klerk.

On the morning of 13 December I was again taken to Tuynhuys. I met de Klerk in the same room where I had had tea with his predecessor. He was accompanied by Kobie

Coetsee, General Willemse, Dr Barnard and his colleague Mike Louw. I congratulated Mr de Klerk on becoming president and expressed the hope that we would be able to work together. He was extremely cordial and reciprocated these sentiments.

From the first I noticed that Mr de Klerk listened to what I had to say. This was a novel experience. National Party leaders generally heard what they wanted to hear in discussions with black leaders, but Mr de Klerk seemed to be making a real attempt to listen and understand.

On 2 February 1990 F. W. de Klerk stood before Parliament to make the traditional opening speech and did something no other South African head of state had ever done: he truly began to dismantle the apartheid system and lay the groundwork for a democratic South Africa. In dramatic fashion, he announced the lifting of the bans on the ANC, the PAC, the South African Communist Party and thirty-one other illegal organizations; the freeing of political prisoners incarcerated for non-violent activities; the suspension of capital punishment; and the lifting of various restrictions imposed by the State of Emergency. 'The time for negotiation has arrived,' he said.

It was a breathtaking moment, for in one sweeping action he had virtually normalized the situation in South Africa. After forty years of persecution and banishment, the ANC was now a legal organization. The international community applauded de Klerk's bold actions. Amid all the good news, however, the ANC objected to the fact that Mr de Klerk had not

completely lifted the State of Emergency or ordered the troops out of the townships.

On 9 February, seven days after Mr de Klerk's speech opening Parliament, I was informed that I was again going to Tuynhuys. I arrived at six o'clock in the evening. I met a smiling Mr de Klerk in his office and, as we shook hands, he informed me that he was going to release me from prison the following day. Although the press in South Africa and around the world had been speculating for weeks that my release was imminent, the announcement nevertheless came as a surprise.

On 2 February 1990 F. W. de Klerk announced the lifting of the ban on the ANC.

I felt a conflict. I deeply wanted to leave prison as soon as I could, but to do so on such short notice would not be wise. I thanked Mr de Klerk, and then said that at the risk of appearing ungrateful I would prefer to have a week's notice in order that my family and my organization could be prepared for my release. Simply to walk out tomorrow, I said, would cause chaos. I asked de Klerk to release me a week from that day. After waiting twenty-seven years, I could certainly wait another seven days.

De Klerk was taken aback. He said that the government would fly me to Johannesburg and officially release me there. I told him that I wanted to walk out of the gates of Victor Verster and be able to thank those who looked after me and greet the people of Cape Town. Though I was from Johannesburg, Cape Town had been my home for nearly three decades. I would make my way back to Johannesburg, but when I chose to, not when the government wanted me to. It was a tense moment and, at the time, neither of us saw any irony in a prisoner asking not be released and his jailer attempting to release him.

De Klerk left the room and returned with a compromise: yes, I could be released at Victor Verster, but, no, the release could not be postponed. The government had already informed the foreign press that I was to be set free the next day and felt they could not renege on that statement. In the end, we agreed on the compromise.

I did not get back to my cottage until shortly before midnight, whereupon I immediately sent word to my colleagues in Cape Town that I was to be released the following day. I managed to get a message to Winnie, and telephoned Walter in Johannesburg. They would all fly in on a chartered plane the next day. That evening, a number of ANC people on what was known as the National Reception Committee came to the cottage to draft a statement that I would make the following day. They left in the early hours of the morning and, despite my excitement, I had no trouble falling asleep.

Freedom

I awoke on the day of my release after only a few hours' sleep. I did a shortened version of my usual exercise regimen, washed and ate breakfast. I then telephoned a number of people from the ANC and the UDF in Cape Town to come to the cottage to prepare for my release and work on my speech. The prison doctor came by to give me a brief check-up. I did not dwell on the prospect of my release, but on all the many things I had to do before then. As so often happens in life, the momentousness of an occasion is lost in the welter of a thousand details.

My actual release time was set for 3 p.m., but Winnie and Walter and the other passengers from the chartered flight from Johannesburg did not arrive until after two. There were already dozens of people at the house, and the entire scene took on the aspect of a celebration.

As we entered the outskirts of the city, I could see people streaming towards the centre. The Reception Committee had organized a rally at the Grand Parade in Cape Town, a great open square that stretched out in front of the old City Hall. We had heard sketchy reports that a great sea of people had been waiting there since morning. I walked out on to the balcony and saw a boundless sea of people cheering, holding flags and banners, clapping and laughing.

I raised my fist, and the crowd responded with an enormous cheer. '*Amandla!*' I called out. '*Ngawethu!*' they responded. '*iAfrika!*' I yelled; '*Mayibuye!*' they answered.

I spoke from the heart. I wanted first of all to tell the people that I was not a messiah, but an ordinary man who had become a leader because of extraordinary circumstances. I wanted immediately to thank the people all over the world who had campaigned for my release. I also publicly expressed my gratitude to my wife and family.

At first I could not really make out what was going on, but when I was within 150 feet or so, I saw a great crowd of people: hundreds of photographers and television cameras and newspeople as well as several thousand well-wishers. I was astounded and a little alarmed. When I was among the crowd I raised my right fist, and there was a roar. I had not been able to do that for twenty-seven years and it gave me a surge of strength and joy.

As I finally walked through those gates I felt – even at the age of seventy-one – that my life was beginning anew. My ten thousand days of imprisonment were at last over.

The following morning we flew by helicopter to the First National Bank stadium in Soweto where I addressed an enormous crowd. We were able to make an aerial tour of Soweto, the teeming metropolis of matchbox houses, tin shanties and dirt roads, the mother city of black urban South Africa, the only home I ever knew as a man before I went to prison. While Soweto had grown, and in some places prospered, the overwhelming majority of the people remained dreadfully poor, without electricity or running water, eking out an existence that was shameful in a nation as wealthy as South Africa. In many places, the poverty was far worse than when I went to prison.

I told the crowd that apartheid had no future in South Africa, and that the people must not scale down their campaign of mass action. 'The sight of freedom looming on the horizon should encourage us to redouble our efforts.' I encouraged the people to return to the barricades, to intensify the struggle, and we would walk the last mile together.

I held a press conference the afternoon after my release. I told the reporters that there was no contradiction between my continuing support for the armed struggle and my advocating negotiations. It was the reality and the threat of the armed struggle that had brought the government to the verge of negotiations. I added that when the state stopped inflicting violence on the ANC, the ANC would reciprocate with peace. Asked about sanctions, I said the ANC could not yet call for the relaxation of sanctions, because the situation that caused sanctions in the first place — the absence of political rights for blacks

— was still the status quo. I might be out of jail, I said, but I was not yet free.

I was asked as well about the fears of whites. I knew that people expected me to harbour anger towards whites. But I had none. I wanted to impress upon the reporters the critical role of whites in any new dispensation. We did not want to destroy the country before we freed it, and to drive the whites away would devastate the nation. I said that there was a middle ground between white fears and black hopes, and we in the ANC would find it. 'Whites are fellow South Africans,' I said, 'and we want them to feel safe and to know that we appreciate the contribution that they have made towards the development of this country.' We must do everything we could to persuade our white compatriots that a new, non-racial South Africa would be a better place for all.

Winnie and I had hoped to spend a few days in Cape Town relaxing, but the people of Johannesburg were getting restless and there might be chaos if I did not return at once. We flew to Johannesburg that evening.

The First National Bank stadium was so crowded that it looked as though it would burst. I expressed my delight to be back among them, but I then scolded the people for some of the crippling problems of urban black life. Students, I said, must return to school. Crime must be brought under control. I told them that I had heard of criminals masquerading as freedom fighters, harassing innocent people and setting alight vehicles; these rogues had no place in the struggle. Freedom without civility, freedom without the ability to live in peace, was not true freedom at all.

I ended by opening my arms to all South Africans of goodwill and good intentions, saying that 'no man or woman who has abandoned apartheid will be excluded from our movement towards a non-racial, united and democratic South Africa based on one-person one-vote on a common voters' roll.' It was the dream I cherished when I entered prison at the age of forty-four, but I was no longer a young man, I was seventy-one, and I could not afford to waste any time.

My first responsibility was to report to the leadership of the ANC, and on 27 February I flew to Lusaka for a meeting of the National Executive Committee. It was a wonderful reunion with old comrades whom I had not seen in decades. A number of African heads of state were also in attendance, and I had brief talks with Robert Mugabe of Zimbabwe, Kenneth Kaunda of Zambia, Quett Masire of Botswana, Joaquim Chissano of Mozambique, José Eduardo Dos Santos of Angola, and Yoweri Museveni of Uganda.

While the members of the Executive were pleased that I had been freed, they were also eager to evaluate the man who had been released. Was Mandela the same man who went to prison twenty-seven years before, or was this a reformed Mandela? Had he survived or had he been broken? They had heard reports of my conversations with the government and they were rightly concerned.

I carefully explained the nature of my talks with the government. I described the demands I had made, and the progress that had been achieved. They had seen the memoranda I had written to Botha and de Klerk, and knew that these documents adhered to ANC policy.

At that session I was elected deputy president of the organization while Alfred Nzo, the organization's secretary-general, was named acting president while Oliver was recuperating from his stroke. At a press conference after our meeting, I was asked about a suggestion made by Dr Kaunda, that the ANC should suspend armed operations inside South Africa now that I had been released. I replied that it was too soon to suspend the armed struggle, for we had not yet achieved the goal for which we had taken up arms.

After a quick tour of Africa, I flew to Stockholm to visit Oliver. Seeing my old friend and law partner was the reunion I most looked forward to. Oliver was not well, but when we met we were like two young boys in the veld who took strength from our love for each other. The first subject he raised was the leadership of the organization. 'Nelson,' he said, 'you must now take over as president of the ANC. I have been merely keeping the job warm for you.' I refused. 'You have been elected by the organization as the president,' I said. 'Let us wait for an election; then the organization can decide.' Oliver protested, but I would not budge.

Chief Buthelezi (right) and King Goodwill Zwelithini (centre) in traditional Zulu dress with supporters of the Inkatha Freedom Party..

Chief Buthelezi, head of the Inkatha Freedom Party and the chief minister of KwaZulu, was one of the premier players on the South African political stage. But within ANC circles, he

was a far from popular figure. As a young man, he had joined the ANC Youth League. I saw him as one of the movement's upcoming young leaders. He had become chief minister of the KwaZulu homeland with the tacit support of the ANC, and even his launching of Inkatha as a Zulu cultural organization was unopposed by the organization. But, over the years, Chief Buthelezi drifted away from the ANC. Though he resolutely opposed apartheid and refused to allow KwaZulu to become an 'independent' homeland as the government wished, he was a thorn in the side of the democratic movement. He opposed the armed struggle. He criticized the 1976 Soweto uprising. He campaigned against international sanctions. Yet Chief Buthelezi had consistently called for my release.

My inclination was to meet the chief as soon as possible to try to resolve our differences. During my initial visit to Lusaka I brought up the idea of such a meeting, and it was voted down. While I was at Victor Verster, Walter had been invited by the Zulu king, Goodwill Zwelithini, to visit him in Ulundi, KwaZulu's capital, and I urged him to accept. I thought it was an excellent opportunity to influence the head of one of the most respected and powerful royal families in the country. The visit was approved by the NEC, provided Walter went to the king's palace in Nongoma; it was thought that going to Ulundi would suggest recognition of the authority of the homeland.

I phoned both Chief Buthelezi and the king, and explained that Walter would be coming to see the king in Nongoma. The king said he would not accept Walter coming to see him anywhere but in the capital. 'Your Majesty,' I said, 'we are facing a wall of opposition from our membership who did not want Mr Sisulu to go to KwaZulu at all. We managed to get this compromise approved; surely you can bend as well?' But he refused to see Walter.

Relations deteriorated after this, and in May I persuaded the ANC of the need for me to make a visit to the king and Buthelezi. The king approved, but a week or so before the visit I received a letter from him to say I must come alone. This proved to be the last straw, and the NEC would not give in to such a demand. I told the king that I could not come unless I was accompanied by my colleagues; the king regarded this as another slight and cancelled the visit.

My goal was to forge an independent relationship with the king, separate from my relationship with Chief Buthelezi. The king was the true hereditary leader of the Zulus, who loved and respected him. Fidelity to the king was far more widespread in KwaZulu than allegiance to Inkatha.

In the meantime, Natal became a killing-ground. Heavily armed Inkatha supporters had in effect declared war on ANC strongholds across the Natal Midlands region and around Pietermaritzburg. Entire villages were set alight, dozens of people were killed, hundreds were wounded and thousands became refugees. In February, only two weeks after my release, I went to Durban and spoke to a crowd of over 100,000 people at King's Park, almost all of whom were Zulus. I pleaded with them to lay down their arms. But my call fell on deaf ears. The fighting and dying continued.

Inkatha supporters had in effect declared war on ANC strongholds across the Natal Midlands region.

I was so concerned that I was willing to go to great lengths to meet Chief Buthelezi. In March, after one particularly horrifying spasm of violence, I announced that I would meet him at a mountain hamlet outside Pietermaritzburg. But the ANC leaders in Natal vetoed my meeting.

In March, we scheduled our first meeting with Mr de Klerk and the government. These were to be 'talks about talks', and were to begin in early April. But on 26 March, in Sebokeng township, about thirty miles south of Johannesburg, the police opened fire without warning on a crowd of ANC demonstrators, killing twelve and wounding hundreds more, most of them shot in the back as they were fleeing. After consultation with the NEC, I announced the suspension of our talks and warned Mr de Klerk that he could not 'talk about negotiations on the one hand and murder our people on the other'.

But with the approval of the leadership, I met privately with Mr de Klerk in Cape Town in order to keep up the momentum for negotiations. Our discussions centred primarily on a new date, and we agreed on early May.

The first round of talks with the government was held over three days in early May. Our delegation consisted of Walter Sisulu, Joe Slovo, Alfred Nzo, Thabo Mbeki, Ahmed Kathrada, Joe Modise, Ruth Mompati, Archie Gumede, the Reverend Beyers Naude, Cheryl Carolus and me. The very fact of the talks themselves was a milestone in the history of our country.

At the end of the three-day meeting, we agreed on what became known as the Groote Schuur Minute, pledging both sides to a peaceful process of negotiations and committing the government to lifting the State of Emergency, which they shortly did everywhere except for the violence-ridden province of Natal.

When it came to constitutional issues, we told the government we were demanding an elected constituent assembly to draw up a new constitution. But before the election of an assembly, it was necessary to have an interim government that could oversee the transition until a new government was elected. The government could not be both player and referee, as it was now.

Although I had wanted to go to Qunu immediately after my release from prison, it was not until April that I was able to travel. I could not pick up and leave whenever I wanted; security had to be arranged, as well as speeches prepared for local organizations. But what was foremost in my mind and heart was paying my respects to my mother's grave.

I went first to Qunu and the site where my mother was buried. I find it difficult to

The setting for the talks was Groote Schuur, (left) the Cape-Dutch-style mansion that was the residence of South Africa's first colonial governors. Some of our delegation joked that we were being led into an ambush on the enemy's ground. But the talks, contrary to expectation, were conducted with seriousness and good humour. Historic enemies who had been fighting each other for three centuries met and shook hands. The government had granted temporary indemnities to Joe Slovo, the general secretary of the Communist Party, and Joe Modise, the commander of MK, and to see these two men shaking hands with the National Party leaders who had demonized them for decades was extraordinary.

describe my feelings: I felt regret that I had been unable to be with her when she died, remorse that I had not been able to look after her properly during her life and a longing for what might have been had I chosen to live my life differently.

In seeing my village again after so many years, I was greatly struck by what had changed and what had not. What had endured was the warmth and simplicity of the community, which took me back to my days as a boy. But what disturbed me was that the villagers seemed as poor if not poorer than they had been then. Most people still lived in simple huts with dirt floors, with no electricity and no running water. When I was young, the village was tidy, the water pure and the grass green and unsullied as far as the eye could see. Kraals were swept, the topsoil was conserved, fields were neatly divided. But now the village was unswept, the water polluted and the countryside littered with plastic bags and wrappers. Pride in the community seemed to have vanished.

In early June I was scheduled to leave on a six-week tour of Europe and North America. Before going, I privately met Mr de Klerk, who asked me to modify the call for the continuation of international sanctions. While we were mindful of what Mr de Klerk had done, in our view sanctions remained the best lever to force him to do more. I explained to Mr de Klerk that we could not tell our supporters to do so until he had completely dismantled apartheid and a transitional government was in place. While he was disappointed at my response, he was not surprised.

The first leg of the trip took Winnie and me to Paris, where we were treated in very grand style by François Mitterrand and his charming wife Danielle, a long-time ANC supporter. This was not my first trip to the continental mainland, but I was still entranced by the beauties of the Old World. While I was in France the government announced the suspension of the State of Emergency. I was pleased, but well aware that they had taken this action while I was in Europe in order to undermine my call for sanctions.

After stops in Switzerland, Italy and the Netherlands, I went to England, where I spent two days on a visit to Oliver and Adelaide. My next stop was the United States. I had read about New York City, and finally to see it from the bottom of its great glass-and-concrete canyons while millions upon millions of pieces of ticker tape came floating down was a breathtaking experience. It was reported that as many as a million people personally witnessed our procession through the city, and to see the support and enthusiasm they gave to the anti-apartheid struggle was truly humbling.

The following day I went to Harlem which, as my wife said, was the Soweto of

Winnie and I ride the 'Mandelamobile' past hundreds of thousands of New Yorkers who lined the streets of Lower Manhattan for a ticker-tape parade in our honour on 20 June 1990.

In London, Mrs Thatcher gave me a stern but well-meaning lecture. 'You must cut your schedule in half,' she said, 'if you keep this up, you will not come out of America alive.'

America. I spoke to a great crowd at Yankee Stadium, telling them that an unbreakable umbilical cord connected black South Africans and black Americans, for together we were children of Africa.

I went to Washington to address a joint session of Congress and attend a private meeting with President Bush. I thanked the US Congress for its anti-apartheid legislation and said the new South Africa hoped to live up to the values that had created the two chambers before which I spoke. I also delivered a strong message on sanctions, for I knew that the Bush administration felt it was time to loosen them. I urged Congress not to do so.

From the United States I proceeded to Canada, where I had a meeting with Prime Minister Mulroney and also addressed their Parliament. Ireland was our next stop, after which I went to London, where I had a three-hour meeting with Mrs Thatcher. She was always a forthright and solicitous lady but I could not make the slightest bit of headway on the question of sanctions.

The government introduced a regulation permitting Zulus to carry so-called 'traditional weapons' to political rallies and meetings. This gave me grave doubts about Mr de Klerk's peaceful intentions.

When I returned to South Africa in July, I requested a meeting with Mr de Klerk. Violence in the country was worsening; the death toll in 1990 was already over fifteen hundred, more than all the political deaths of the previous year. Our country was bleeding to death, and we had to move ahead faster.

In July, shortly before a scheduled meeting of the National Executive Committee, Joe Slovo came to me privately with a proposition. He suggested we voluntarily suspend the armed struggle in order to create the right climate to move the negotiation process forward. Mr de Klerk, he said, needed to show his supporters that his policy had brought benefits to the country. My first reaction was negative. But the more I thought about it, the more I realized that we had to take the initiative. I also recognized that Joe, whose credentials as a radical were above dispute, was the right person to make the proposal. He could not be accused of being a dupe of the government or of having gone soft. The following day I told Joe that if he brought up the idea in the NEC, I would support him.

On 6 August in Pretoria, the ANC and the government signed what became known as the Pretoria Minute in which we agreed to suspend the armed struggle. The agreement also set forth target dates for the release of political prisoners and the granting of certain types of indemnity. The government also agreed to review the Internal Security Act.

Of all the issues that hindered the peace process, none was more devastating and frustrating than the escalation of violence in the country. We had all hoped that as negotiations got under way, violence would decrease. But in fact the opposite happened. The police and security forces were making very few arrests. People in the townships were accusing them of aiding and abetting the violence. It was becoming more and more clear to me that there was connivance on the part of the security forces.

Over the next few months, I visited townships all across the violence-racked Vaal Triangle south of Johannesburg. Over and over again I heard the same story: the police and the defence force were destabilizing the area.

In September I gave a speech in which I said there was a hidden hand behind the violence and suggested that there was a mysterious 'Third Force', which consisted of renegade men from the security forces who were attempting to disrupt the negotiations.

During this time, the government took another action that added fuel to the flames. It introduced a regulation permitting Zulus to carry so-called 'traditional weapons' to political rallies and meetings in Natal and elsewhere. These weapons, assegais, which are spears, and knobkerries, wooden sticks with a heavy wooden head, are actual weapons with which Inkatha members killed ANC members. This gave me grave doubts about Mr de Klerk's peaceful intentions.

As the violence continued to spiral, I began to have second thoughts about the suspension of the armed struggle. In September, at a press conference, I said that the

Oliver Tambo returns to South Africa. During the twenty-seven years that I was in prison, it was Oliver who saved the ANC and then built it up into an international organization with power and influence.

continuing violence might necessitate taking up arms once more. The situation looked very grim, and any understanding that had been achieved with the government seemed lost.

In December 1990 Oliver returned to South Africa, having been in exile for three decades. It was wonderful to have him near. He returned for an ANC consultative conference in Johannesburg, which was attended by over fifteen hundred delegates from forty-five different regions, from home and abroad. At the meeting I spoke in tribute to Oliver as the man who had led the ANC during its darkest hours and never let the flame go out. Now, he had ushered us to the brink of a future that looked bright and hopeful.

In July 1991 the ANC held its first annual conference inside South Africa in thirty years. At the conference I was elected president of the ANC without opposition. Cyril Ramaphosa was elected secretary-general, evidence that the torch was being passed from an older generation of leadership to a younger one.

In my speech I expressed my appreciation for the great honour that had been bestowed on me, and spoke of how difficult it would be to follow in the great footsteps of my predecessor, Oliver Tambo. Though we were then at loggerheads with the government, negotiations in themselves constituted a victory.

On 20 December 1991, after more than a year and a half of talks about talks, the real talks began: CODESA – the Convention for a Democratic South Africa – represented the first formal negotiations forum between the government, the ANC and other South African parties. The talks took place at the World Trade Centre in Johannesburg. CODESA comprised eighteen delegations covering the gamut of South African politics, plus observers from the United Nations, the Commonwealth, the European Community and the Organization of African Unity. It was the widest cross-section of political groups ever gathered in one place in South Africa.

On the convention's first day, the lion's share of the participating parties, including the National Party and the ANC, endorsed a Declaration of Intent, which committed all parties to support an undivided South Africa whose supreme law would be a constitution safeguarded by an independent judiciary. The country's legal system would guarantee equality before the law, and a bill of rights would be drawn up to protect civil liberties. In short there would be a multi-party democracy based on universal adult suffrage on a common voters' roll.

The first day of CODESA 1 was uneventful. At the end of the session, all seemed well; I spoke about the importance of the talks and I was followed by Mr de Klerk. He underlined the historic significance of the occasion and discussed the need for overcoming mutual distrust. But he then began to attack the ANC for not adhering to the agreements that we had made with the government. He berated the ANC for failing to disclose the location of arms caches and for maintaining a 'private army', Umkhonto we Sizwe, in

As **CODESA** talks open, demonstrators in Cape Town burn posters of Verwoerd, Vorster and P. W. de Klerk.

violation of the National Peace Accord of September 1991. He questioned whether the ANC was honourable enough to abide by any agreements it signed.

This was more than I could tolerate. I said it was unacceptable for Mr de Klerk to speak to us in such language. I reiterated that it was the ANC, not the government, that started the initiative of peace discussions, and it was the government, not the ANC, who time and again failed to live up to its agreements. I noted that we had suspended our armed struggle to show our commitment to peace, yet the government was still colluding with those waging war. We told him that we would turn in our weapons only when we were a part of the government collecting those weapons, and not until then.

It was apparent the government had a double agenda. They were using the negotiations not to achieve peace, but to score their own petty political gains. Even while negotiating, they were secretly funding covert organizations that committed violence against us. I mentioned the recent revelations about million-rand pay-offs to Inkatha that Mr de Klerk claimed not to have known about. I stated that if a man in his position 'doesn't know about such things, then he is not fit to be the head of government'.

CODESA convened the following day for its final session, and both Mr de Klerk and I took pains to show that no irreparable harm had been done. He and I publicly shook hands and said we would work together. But much trust had been lost, and the negotiations were now in a state of disarray.

Six weeks after the opening of CODESA 1, the National Party contested an important by-election in Potchefstroom, a conservative university town in the Transvaal, traditionally the party's stronghold. In a stunning upset, the Nationalists were defeated by the candidate of the right-wing Conservative Party. The Conservatives resolutely opposed the government's policy of negotiations with the ANC, and were composed mainly of Afrikaners who felt that Mr de Klerk was giving away the store.

Mr de Klerk decided to gamble. He announced that as a result of the by-election in Potchefstroom he would call a nationwide all-white referendum for 17 March in order to vote on his reform policy and on negotiations with the ANC. He stated that if the referendum was defeated, he would resign from office. In the end, 69 per cent of the white voters supported negotiations, giving de Klerk a great victory. His hand was strengthened, and as a result, the Nationalists toughened their negotiating positions.

On 13 April 1992 at a press conference in Johannesburg, flanked by my two oldest friends and comrades, Walter and Oliver, I announced my separation from my wife. The situation had grown so difficult that I felt that it was in the best interests of all concerned – the ANC, the family and Winnie – that we part. Although I discussed the matter with the ANC, the separation itself was made for personal reasons.

In May 1992 the multi-party conference held its second plenary session at the World Trade Centre. Known as CODESA 2, the talks had been prepared by secret meetings between

❝ That night, I returned with Winnie to No. 8115 in Orlando West. It was only then that I knew in my heart that I had left prison. For me, No. 8115 was the centrepoint of my world, the place marked with an X in my mental geography. The four-roomed house had been soundly rebuilt after the fire. When I saw it, I was surprised by how much smaller and humbler it was than I remembered it being. Compared with my cottage at Victor Verster, No. 8115 could have been the servants' quarters at the back. But any house in which a man is free is a castle when compared with even the plushest prison. ❞

negotiators from both the ANC and the government as well as discussions between the ANC and other parties.

Only days before CODESA 2 was to begin, the government was hit by two scandals. The first involved the revelation of massive corruption and bribery at the Department of Development Aid, which was responsible for improving black life in the homelands, and the second was the implication of high government security officials in the 1985 murder of four of the UDF, the best known of whom was Matthew Goniwe. These two scandals undermined the credibility of the government and strengthened our hand.

The ANC and government teams had put together a tentative agreement involving a two-stage transitional period to a fully democratic South Africa. In the first stage, a multi-party 'transitional executive council' would be appointed from the CODESA delegations to function as a temporary government in order to 'level the playing-field' for all parties and create an interim constitution. In the second stage, general elections would be held for a constituent assembly and legislature in which all political parties winning 5 per cent or more of the vote would participate in the cabinet. Half the members of the assembly would be elected on a national basis and half on a regional one, and the assembly would be empowered both to write a new constitution and to pass legislation. An independent commission would preside over the election and make sure it was free and fair.

Yet there were many matters on which the ANC and the government could not reach agreement, such as the percentage of voting necessary in the assembly to decide constitutional issues and to agree on a bill of rights. Only days before CODESA 2, the government proposed a second body, a senate, composed of regional representatives, as a way of ensuring a minority veto. They also proposed that, before all this, CODESA 2 first agree on an interim constitution, which would take months to draw up.

All of this bargaining was going on behind the scenes, and by the time CODESA 2 opened on 15 May 1992, the prospects for agreement looked bleak.

The convention was deadlocked at the end of the first day. At that time, the two judges presiding over the talks told Mr de Klerk and me to meet that evening to attempt to find a compromise. We decided that we would each speak the following day in a spirit of constructive compromise. But the convention ended the second day in a stalemate. The impasse, as I saw it, was caused by the National Party's continuing reluctance to submit their fate to the will of the majority. They simply could not cross that hurdle.

With negotiations stalled, the ANC and its allies agreed on a policy of 'rolling mass action', which would display to the government the extent of our support around the country. The mass action consisted of strikes, demonstrations and boycotts. The date chosen for the start of mass action was 16 June 1992, the anniversary of the 1976 Soweto revolt.

But before that happened, another event occurred that drove the ANC and the government even further apart. On the night of 17 June 1992, a heavily armed force of Inkatha members secretly raided the Vaal township of Boipatong and killed forty-six

On 17 June 1992 a heavily armed force of Inkatha members raided the Vaal township of Boipatong and killed forty-six people. Most of the dead were women and children.

people. It was the fourth mass killing of ANC people that week. People across the country were horrified by the violence and charged the government with complicity. The police did nothing to stop the criminals and no arrests were made. Mr de Klerk said nothing. I found this to be the last straw. The government was blocking the negotiations and at the same time waging a covert war against our people. Why then were we continuing to talk with them?

Four days after the murders, I addressed a crowd of twenty thousand angry ANC supporters and told them I had instructed the ANC secretary-general Cyril Ramaphosa to suspend direct dealings with the government. It was as if we had returned to the dark days of Sharpeville. I publicly warned de Klerk that if he sought to impose new measures to restrict demonstrations or free expression, the ANC would launch a nationwide defiance campaign with myself as the first volunteer.

The mass action campaign culminated in a general strike on 3 and 4 August in support

of the ANC's negotiation demands and in protest against state-supported violence. More than four million workers stayed at home in what was the largest political strike in South African history.

In the face of this mass action, Mr de Klerk said that if the ANC made the country ungovernable, the government might be forced to consider some unpleasant options. I warned Mr de Klerk that any anti-democratic actions would have serious repercussions. It was because of such threats, I said, that it was absolutely critical to set up a transitional government.

Inspired by the success of the mass action campaign, a group within the ANC decided to march on Bisho, the capital of the Ciskei homeland in the eastern Cape. The Ciskei had a history of repression against the ANC. On the morning of 7 September 1992, seventy thousand protesters set out on a march to Bisho's main stadium. The poorly trained homeland troops opened fire on the marchers and killed twenty-nine people, wounding over two hundred. Now Bisho joined Boipatong as a byword for brutality.

Like the old proverb that says the darkest hour is before the dawn, the tragedy of Bisho led to a new opening in the negotiations. I met de Klerk in order to find common ground and avoid another tragedy like Bisho. Both sides were making an effort in good faith to get the negotiations back on track, and on 26 September de Klerk and I met for an official summit. On that day he and I signed the Record of Understanding, an agreement which set the mould for all the negotiations that followed.

The Record of Understanding prompted Inkatha to announce its withdrawal from all negotiations involving the government and the ANC. Chief Buthelezi called for the abolition of the Record of Understanding, the ending of CODESA and the disbanding of Umkhonto we Sizwe.

Joe Slovo again took the lead. He proposed a 'sunset clause' providing for a government of national unity that would include power-sharing with the National Party for a fixed period of time, an amnesty for security officers and the honouring of contracts of civil servants. 'Power-sharing' in this context merely meant that the National Party would be part of any popularly elected government, provided it polled enough votes.

I supported Joe's proposal and it was endorsed by the National Executive on 18 November. In February the ANC and the government announced an agreement in principle on the five-year government of national unity, a multi-party cabinet and the creation of a transitional executive council. Elections would be held as early as the end of 1993.

I have always believed that a man should have a home within sight of the house where he was born. After being released from prison, I set about plans to build a country house for myself in Qunu. I was at my house on a brief holiday when the news came that Chris

Hani, the former chief of staff of MK and one of the most popular figures in the ANC, had been shot in Johannesburg. There were concerns that Hani's death might trigger a racial war, with the youth deciding that their hero should become a martyr for whom they would lay down their own lives.

Later, I learned that the police had arrested a member of the militant right-wing Afrikaner Weerstandsbeweging (AWB). The murder was an act of mad desperation, an attempt to derail the negotiation process. I was asked to speak on the SABC that night to address the nation. In this instance, it was the ANC, not the government, that sought to calm the people.

I said that the process of peace and negotiations could not be halted. With all the authority at my command, I said, 'I appeal to all our people to remain calm and to honour the memory of Chris Hani by remaining a disciplined force for peace.'

Although few people will remember 3 June 1993, it was a landmark in South African history. On that day, after months of negotiations at the World Trade Centre, the multi-party forum voted to set a date for the country's first national, non-racial, one-person-one-vote election: 27 April 1994. For the first time in South African history, the black majority would go to the polls to elect their own leaders. The agreement was that voters would elect four hundred representatives to a constituent assembly, which would both write a new constitution and serve as a parliament. After convening, the first order of business for the assembly would be to elect a president.

The talks had reconvened in April. This time, the twenty-six parties included Inkatha, the Pan-Africanist Congress and the Conservative Party. We had been pressing the government to establish a date for months, and they had been stalling. But now the date was written in stone.

A month later, in July, the multi-party forum agreed on a first draft of an interim constitution. It provided for a bicameral parliament with a four-hundred-member national assembly elected by proportional representation from national and regional party lists, and a senate elected indirectly by regional legislatures.

Chief Buthelezi wanted a constitution drawn up before the election and walked out in protest against the setting of an election date before a constitution was finalized. A second draft interim constitution in August gave greater powers to the regions, but this did not placate either Chief Buthelezi or the Conservative Party. The Conservative Party described the resolutions as hostile to Afrikaner interests. A group called the Afrikaner Volksfront, led by General Constand Viljoen, a former chief of the South African Defence Force, was formed to unite conservative white organizations around the idea of a *volkstaat*, a white homeland.

Just after midnight on 18 November an interim constitution was approved by a plenary session of the multiparty conference. The government and the ANC had cleared the remaining hurdles. The new cabinet would be composed of those winning more than

Chris's death was a blow to me personally and to the movement. He was a soldier and patriot, for whom no task was too small. He was a great hero among the youth of South Africa, a man who spoke their language and to whom they listened. If anyone could mobilize the unruly youth behind a negotiated solution, it was Chris. South Africa was now deprived of one of its greatest sons, a man who would have been invaluable in transforming the country into a new nation.

5 per cent of the vote and would make decisions by consensus, rather than the two-thirds majority proposed by the government; national elections would not take place until 1999, so that the government of national unity would serve for five years; finally, the government gave way on our insistence on a single ballot paper for the election, rather than separate ballots for national and provincial legislatures. Two ballot papers would only confuse a majority of voters, most of whom would be voting for the first time in their lives. In the period leading up to the election, a Transitional Executive Council with members from each party would ensure the right climate for the elections. In effect, the TEC would be the government between 22 December and the election on 27 April. An Independent Electoral Commission with extensive powers would be responsible for the administration of the election.

The official campaign for the national assembly was not scheduled to begin until February 1994, but we started to campaign in earnest after the new constitution was ratified. Although the polls showed the ANC with a healthy margin, I counselled everyone against over-optimism. We faced an experienced, well-organized and well-financed rival.

The first stage of our election effort was what were known as People's Forums. ANC candidates would travel all over the country and hold meetings in towns and villages in order to listen to the hopes and fears, the ideas and complaints, of our people.

After incorporating the suggestions from the forums, we travelled the country delivering our message to the people. We wanted people to vote for the ANC not simply because we had fought apartheid for eighty years, but because we were best qualified to bring about the kind of South Africa they hoped to live in.

The ANC drafted a 150-page document known as the Reconstruction and Development Programme, which outlined our plan to create jobs through public works; to build a million new houses with electricity and flush toilets; to extend primary health care and provide ten years of free education to all South Africans; to redistribute land through a land claims court; and to end the value-added tax on basic foodstuffs. We were also committed to extensive affirmative action measures in both the private and public sectors. This document was translated into a simpler manifesto called 'A Better Life for All', which in turn became the ANC's campaign slogan.

The first stage of our election effort was what were known as People's Forums. The forums were parliaments of the people, not unlike the meetings of chiefs at the Great Place that I witnessed as a boy.

I felt we must also tell them what we could not do. Many people felt life would change overnight after a free and democratic election, but that would be far from the case. 'You must have patience,' I told them. 'You might have to wait five years for results to show.'

I told white audiences that we needed them and did not want them to leave the country. They were South Africans just like ourselves and this was their land, too. I said, over and over, that we should forget the past and concentrate on building a better future for all.

12 February 1994 was the deadline for registration of all parties, and on that day Inkatha, the Conservative Party and the Afrikaner Volksfront failed to sign. The government of the Bophuthatswana homeland also refused to participate and resisted reincorporation into a united South Africa. I was disturbed that these important groups were choosing not to participate. To bring them on board, we proposed certain significant compromises: we agreed to the use of double ballots for provincial and national legislatures; guarantees of greater provincial powers; the renaming of Natal province as KwaZulu/Natal; and the affirmation that a principle of 'internal' self-determination would be included in the constitution for groups sharing a common cultural and language heritage.

I arranged to meet Chief Buthelezi in Durban on 1 March. 'I will go down on my knees to beg those who want to drag our country into bloodshed,' I told a rally before this meeting. Chief Buthelezi agreed to register provisionally for the elections in exchange for a promise to subject our differences over constitutional issues to international mediation. To this I gladly assented. Before the final registration deadline, General Viljoen also registered under a new party known as the Freedom Front.

Though Lucas Mangope, the president of Bophuthatswana, had chosen to keep his homeland out of the election, the tide of events soon altered the situation. Those who wanted to participate launched mass demonstrations and strikes, which soon spread to the

Bophuthatswana civil service. Battles broke out between the homeland police and striking workers and students. Mangope called in military help from his white right-wing allies. Soon his own forces deserted him and he was ousted in a coup in early March. A few weeks later, Brigadier Gqozo in the Ciskei capitulated and asked South Africa to take over the homeland.

Violence in Natal worsened. Inkatha supporters were blocking our efforts to campaign in Natal. In March, Judge Johann Kriegler reported to me and Mr de Klerk that because of the lack of cooperation from the KwaZulu government, free elections could not be held there without direct political intervention. To demonstrate our strength in Natal, the ANC held a mass march through the centre of Durban. Then Inkatha attempted to do the same in Johannesburg, with dire results.

On 28 March thousands of Inkatha members brandishing spears and knobkerries marched through Johannesburg to a rally in the centre of town. At the same time an armed Inkatha group attempted to enter Shell House, the ANC headquarters, but was repulsed by armed guards. Altogether fifty-three people died. It was a grisly spectacle that made South Africa appear as if it was on the brink of internal war. Inkatha was attempting to postpone the election, but neither Mr de Klerk nor I would budge. That day was sacrosanct.

I had agreed to international mediation, and on 13 April a delegation arrived led by Lord Carrington, the former British foreign secretary, and Henry Kissinger, the former American secretary of state. But when Inkatha was informed that the election date was not subject to mediation, they refused to see the mediators, who left without talking to anyone. Now Chief Buthelezi knew the election would take place no matter what. On 19 April Chief Buthelezi accepted the offer of a constitutional role for the Zulu monarchy and agreed to participate.

The images of South Africans going to the polls that day are burned in my memory. Great lines of patient people snaking through the dirt roads and streets of towns and cities; old women who had waited half a century to cast their first vote saying that they felt like human beings for the first time in their lives; white men and women saying they were proud to live in a free country at last. The mood of the nation during those days of voting was buoyant. The violence and bombings ceased, and it was as though we were a nation reborn. Even the logistical difficulties of the voting, misplaced ballots, pirate voting stations and rumours of fraud in certain places could not dim the overwhelming victory for democracy and justice.

Ten days before the vote, Mr de Klerk and I held our single television debate. I accused the National Party of fanning race hatred between Coloureds and Africans in the Cape by distributing an inflammatory comic book that said the ANC's slogan was 'Kill a Coloured, kill a farmer'. 'There is no organization in this country as divisive as the new National Party,' I declared. When Mr de Klerk criticized the ANC's plan to spend billions of dollars on housing and social programmes, I scolded him, saying he was alarmed that we would have to devote so many of our resources to blacks.

But as the debate was nearing an end, I felt I had been too harsh with the man who would be my partner in a government of national unity. 'In spite of criticism of Mr de Klerk,' I said, and then looked over at him, 'sir, you are one of those I rely upon. We are going to face the problem of this country together.' At which point I reached over to take his hand and said, 'I am proud to hold your hand for us to go forward.' Mr de Klerk seemed surprised, but pleased.

Before I entered the polling station, an irreverent member of the press called out, 'Mr Mandela, who are you voting for?' I laughed. 'You know,' I said, 'I have been agonizing over that choice all morning.' I marked an X in the box next to the letters ANC and then slipped my folded ballot paper into a simple wooden box; I had cast the first vote of my life, like the woman pictured above.

I voted on 27 April, the second of the four days of voting. I chose to vote in Natal to show the people in that divided province that there was no danger in going to the polling stations.

It took several days for the results to be counted. We polled 62.6 per cent of the national vote, slightly short of the two-thirds needed had we wished to push through a final constitution without support from other parties.

Some in the ANC were disappointed that we did not cross the two-thirds threshold, but I was not one of them. In fact I was relieved; had we won two-thirds of the vote and been able to write a constitution unfettered by input from others, people would argue that we had created an ANC constitution, not a South African constitution. I wanted a true government of national unity.

On the evening of 2 May Mr de Klerk made a gracious concession speech. After more than three centuries of rule, the white minority was conceding defeat and turning over power to the black majority. That evening the ANC was planning a victory celebration at the ballroom of the Carlton Hotel in downtown Johannesburg. I went on stage at about nine o'clock and faced a crowd of happy, smiling, cheering faces.

From the moment the results were in and it was apparent that the ANC was to form the government, I saw my mission as one of preaching reconciliation. I knew that many people, particularly the minorities, whites, Coloureds and Indians, would be feeling anxious about the future, and I wanted them to feel secure. At every opportunity, I said all South Africans must now unite and join hands and say we are one country, one nation, one people, marching together into the future.

10 May dawned bright and clear. The inauguration would be the largest gathering ever of international leaders on South African soil. On that lovely autumn day I was

The ceremonies took place in the sandstone amphitheatre formed by the Union Buildings in Pretoria. For decades this had been the seat of white supremacy, and now it was the site of a rainbow gathering of different colours and nations for the installation of South Africa's first democratic, non-racial government. On that lovely autumn day I was accompanied by my daughter Zenani.

Foreign dignitaries included Fidel Castro (right), the Duke of Edinburgh (far right), Benazir Bhutto (below right) and Yasser Arafat (below far right).

On the day of the inauguration, I was overwhelmed with a sense of history. In the first decade of the twentieth century, a few years after the bitter Anglo-Boer war and before my own birth, the white-skinned peoples of South Africa patched up their differences and erected a system of racial domination against the dark-skinned peoples of their own land.

The structure they created formed the basis of one of the harshest, most inhumane, societies the world has ever known. Now, in the last decade of the twentieth century, and my own eighth decade as a man, that system had been overturned forever and replaced by one that recognized the rights and freedoms of all peoples regardless of the colour of their skin.

accompanied by my daughter Zenani. On the podium, Mr de Klerk was first sworn in as second deputy president. Then Thabo Mbeki was sworn in as first deputy president. When it was my turn, I pledged to obey and uphold the constitution and to devote myself to the well-being of the republic and its people. The day was symbolized for me by the playing of our two national anthems, and the vision of whites singing 'Nkosi Sikele' iAfrika' and blacks singing 'Die Stem', the old anthem of the republic.

I was not born with a hunger to be free. I was born free – free to run in the fields, free to swim in the stream that ran through my village, free to roast mealies under the stars. As long as I obeyed my father and abided by the customs of my tribe, I was not troubled by the laws of man or God.

It was only when I began to learn that my boyhood freedom was an illusion, when I discovered as a young man that my freedom had already been taken from me, that I began to hunger for it. At first, I wanted the transitory freedoms of being able to stay out at night, read what I pleased and go where I chose. Later, I yearned for the basic freedoms of achieving my potential, of earning my keep, of marrying and having a family.

But then I slowly saw that it was not just my freedom that was curtailed, but the freedom of everyone who looked like I did. That is when I joined the African National Congress, and that is when the hunger for freedom became the greater hunger for the freedom of my people. It was this desire for people to live their lives with dignity and self-respect that animated my life, that transformed a frightened young man into a bold one, that drove a law-abiding attorney to become a criminal, that turned a family-loving husband into a man without a home, that forced a life-loving man to live like a monk.

It was during those long and lonely years that my hunger for the freedom of my own people became a hunger for the freedom of all people, white and black. I knew that the oppressor must be liberated just as surely as the oppressed. When I walked out of prison, that was my mission, to liberate the oppressed and the oppressor both. The truth is that we are not yet free; we have merely achieved the freedom to be free, the right not to be oppressed. We have not taken the final step of our journey, but the first step on a longer and even more difficult road. For to be free is not merely to cast off one's chains, but to live in a way that respects and enhances the freedom of others. The true test of our devotion to freedom is just beginning.

I have walked that long road to freedom. But I have discovered that after climbing a great hill, one only finds that there are many more hills to climb. I have taken a moment here to rest, to steal a view of the glorious vista that surrounds me, to look back on the distance I have come. But I can rest only for a moment, for with freedom come responsibilities, and I dare not linger, for my long walk is not yet ended.

Index

Picture Acknowledgements

The Publishers would like to thank the following individuals and organisations for supplying illustrations:

Archive Photos 121 bottom

Associated Press/Denis Farrell 198–99

Bailey's African History Archives 24, 26, 31, 39, 43, 52, 60, 61, 73,82, 83, 114

Bailey's African History Archives/Bob Gosani 22, 55

Bailey's African History Archives/Jurgen Schadeberg 54

Bailey's African History Archives//Ronnie Manyosi 80

Black Star/Peter Turnley 180

Craig Fraser 28, 183

Thys Ferreira (TK) 203

Fanie Jason 14, 182, 187, 188, 192

Katz Pictures Ltd/Tom Stoddart 179

Katz Pictures/Time Magazine/Peter Magubane/ 202

Magnum Photos/Gideon Mendel 178

Magnum Photos/Ian Berry 200

Mayibuye Centre 8, 16, 17, 23, 25, 32 (both), 33, 34, 35, 36, 37, 38, 42, 45, 47, 49,
50, 51, 58, 59, 62, 66, 68, 69, 71, 74, 76, 78, 79, 85, 86, 87, 89, 92 (both), 95, 97, 98, 99,
100, 101, 103, 104, 109, 112, 113, 115, 117, 120, 121 top, 131, 137, 141, 143 (all three),
147, 151, 152 (both), 153, 160, 161, 162, 175, 186 bottom

Mayibuye Centre/Tony McGrath 63

Mayibuye Centre/Carolin Schuten 27

Mayibuye Centre/Jurgen Schadeberg 67

Mayibuye Centre/Peter Magubane 125

McGregor Museum/Duggan-Cronin Collection 7,10 bottom

McGregor Museum/Jean Morris Collection 6, 9 top

McGregor Museum/Aubrey Elliott Collection 1,9 bottom,21

Mirror Syndication International 185

Museum of Africa 30, 40, 70 top,70 bottom,75 top,75 bottom,77

Network Photographers/Gideon Mendel 196

Photo Access/Walter Knirr 12–13, 56–57

Photo Access/Glynn Griffiths 140

Popperfoto/Reuter 186

Select Photo Agency/Jurgen Schadeberg 46

Schadeberg Movie Company/Jurgen Schadeberg Front cover, 52, 53, 65, 72, 81, 118, 119,
122, 123, 124, 126–7, 128 (both), 133, 134, 135,139,149,150

South African Library, Cape Town 15 (both), 41, 154

Southern Images/Benny Gool 156, 171, 172, 174, 176, 177, 184, 189, 193

Southern Images/G. Hallett 195, 197

Southlight Photo Agency/David Goldblatt 111

Southlight Photo Agency/Paul Weinberg 157, 168, 169

Southlight Photo Agency/Guy Tillim 159, 165, 166

Southlight Photo Agency/Dave Hartman 167

Southlight Photo Agency/Paul Velasco 181, 201 top, centre row middle & right, bottom row both

Southlight Photo Agency/Ellen Elmendorp 201 centre row left

Guy Tillim Back cover (not US edition), 2, 10 top, 11

University of the Witwatersrand, Johannesburg 90, 91 (all four)